Rewiring My Brain: Activities for Aph

Welcome to Rewiring My Brain: Activities for Aphasia Rehabilitation, a comprehensive workbook designed to help individuals recovering from aphasia, regain their writing skills. This workbook provides a variety of exercises aimed at improving handwriting, letter and number recognition, category and word association, as well as overall language comprehension and communication.

The exercises in this workbook are specifically designed to provide individuals recovering from aphasia with a wide range of tools and techniques to help them overcome the challenges of writing and communication. The exercises are arranged in a progressive manner, with each section building on the skills developed in the previous sections. The workbook begins with tracing exercises and progresses to more complex tasks such as divergent naming, analogies, and comprehension.

This workbook is designed for use by individuals recovering from aphasia as well as their caregivers, family members, and therapists. The exercises can be completed individually or with the assistance of a caregiver or therapist. Each exercise provides clear instructions and examples to help guide the user through the process.

Whether you are just beginning your journey towards recovery from aphasia or looking for additional tools and techniques to improve your writing skills, this workbook is designed to provide you with the tools and support you need to succeed. We hope that this workbook serves as a valuable resource in your recovery and helps you on your journey to regain your communication and language skills.

Disclaimer: The exercises in this workbook were created to aid in the rehabilitation of individuals with stroke or aphasia. While the exercises have been designed with the intention of helping patients regain their language and writing abilities, the author of this workbook cannot guarantee specific results or outcomes. It is important to consult with a licensed speech-language pathologist or other qualified healthcare provider for a comprehensive evaluation and personalized treatment plan. The author is not responsible for any results or lack thereof that may occur from the use of this workbook.

Table of Contents

Tracing Exercises

Tracing exercises can be a valuable tool in aphasia recovery for several reasons:

Fine motor skill development: Tracing exercises help improve fine motor skills, which are important for controlling the small movements in the hands and fingers. This can benefit individuals with aphasia who may also have difficulty with writing or other tasks that require precise hand movements.

Visual-spatial processing: Tracing activities require individuals to process visual information and coordinate their hand movements accordingly. This can help improve visual-spatial processing, which is important for understanding the spatial relationships between objects and navigating one's environment.

Attention and focus: Tracing exercises require individuals to pay close attention to the task at hand and maintain focus for an extended period. This can help improve attention and concentration skills, which are important for language processing and communication.

Cognitive stimulation: Engaging in tracing activities can provide cognitive stimulation, which is essential for overall brain health and can help support language recovery in people with aphasia.

Calming effect: Tracing can have a calming effect, helping to reduce stress and anxiety. Lower stress levels can be beneficial for individuals with aphasia, as stress can exacerbate communication difficulties.

Integration with language tasks: Tracing exercises can be integrated with language tasks, such as writing or reading, to help reinforce language skills and support the recovery process. While tracing exercises alone may not directly improve language abilities, they can contribute to the overall recovery process by supporting the development of related skills and providing cognitive stimulation. It's important to incorporate tracing exercises as part of a comprehensive aphasia treatment plan that includes various language and cognitive tasks tailored to the individual's needs.

Tracing

Fine motor skills practice

Tracing

Fine motor skills practice

Tracing

Fine motor skills practice

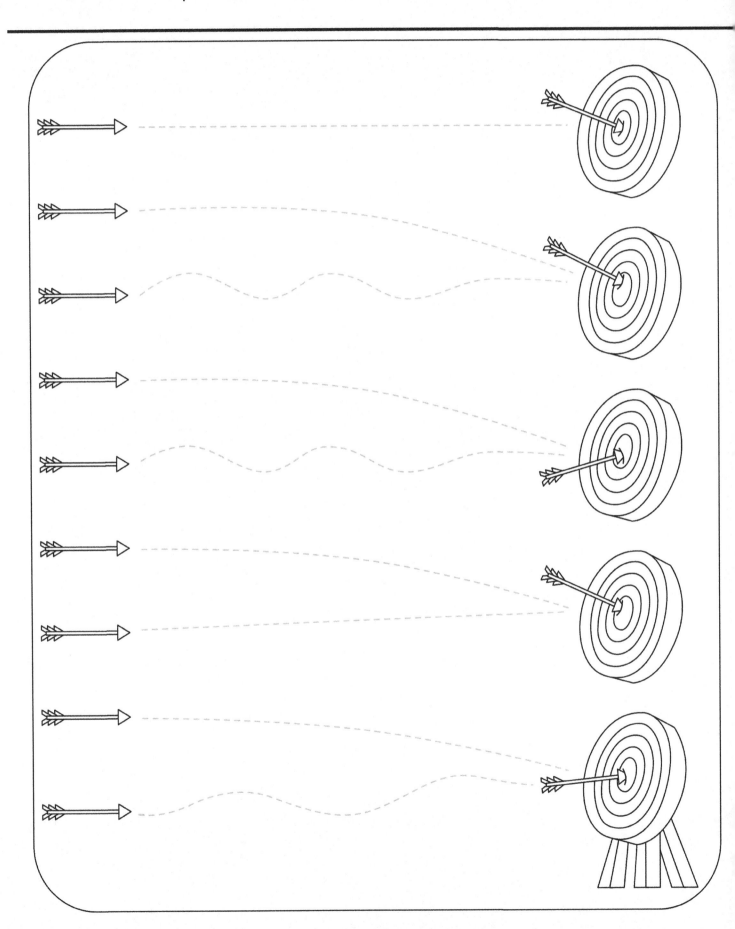

Tracing

Fine motor skills practice

Tracing

Fine motor skills practice

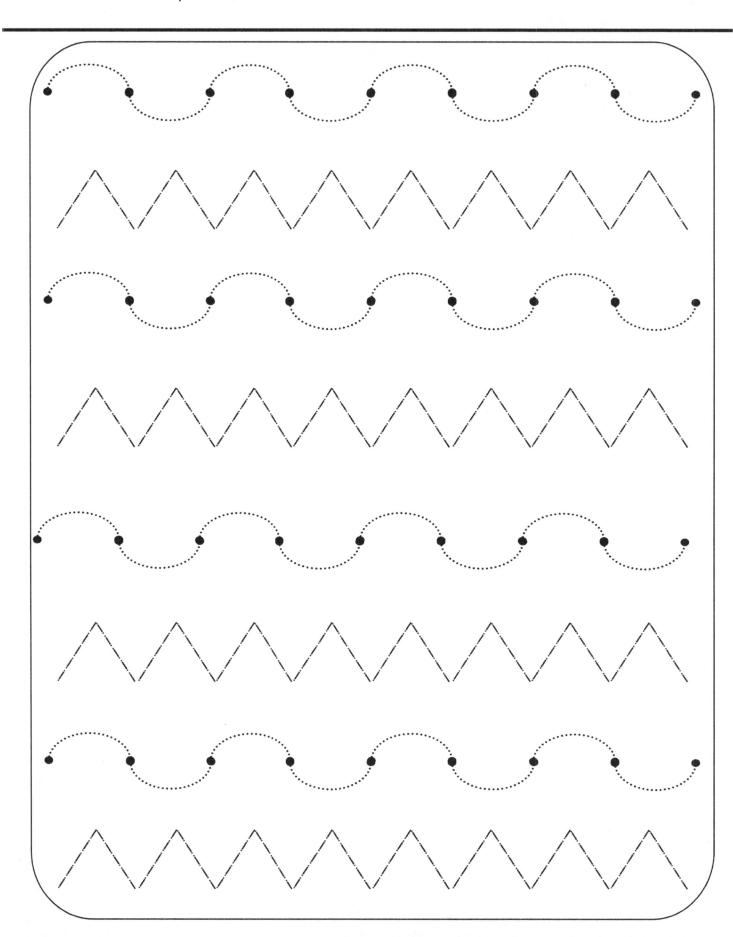

Tracing
Fine motor skills practice

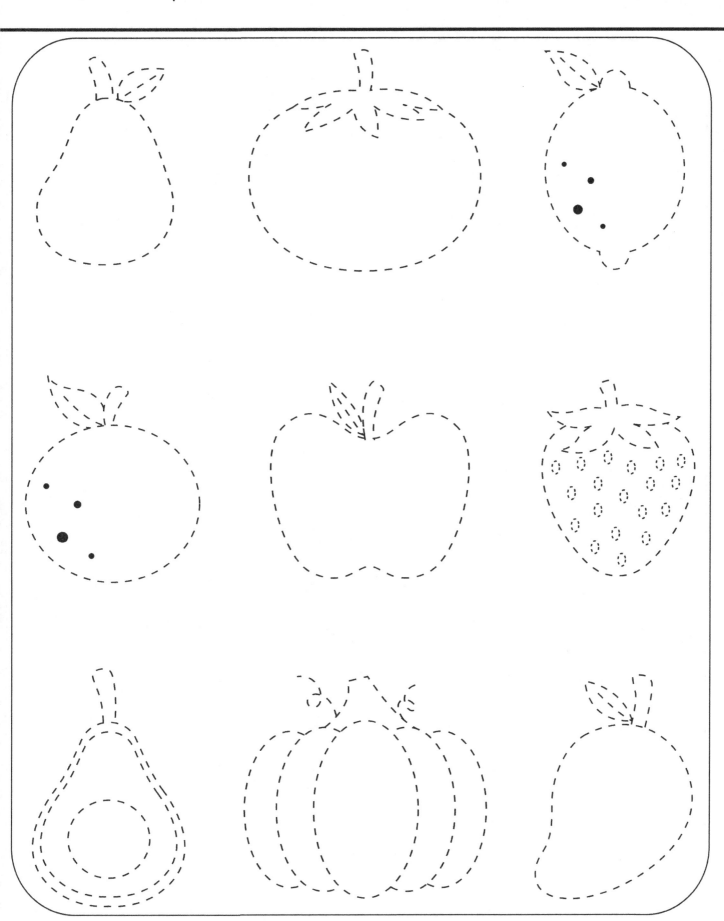

Tracing

Fine motor skills practice

Tracing
Fine motor skills practice

Tracing

Fine motor skills practice

Tracing

Fine motor skills practice

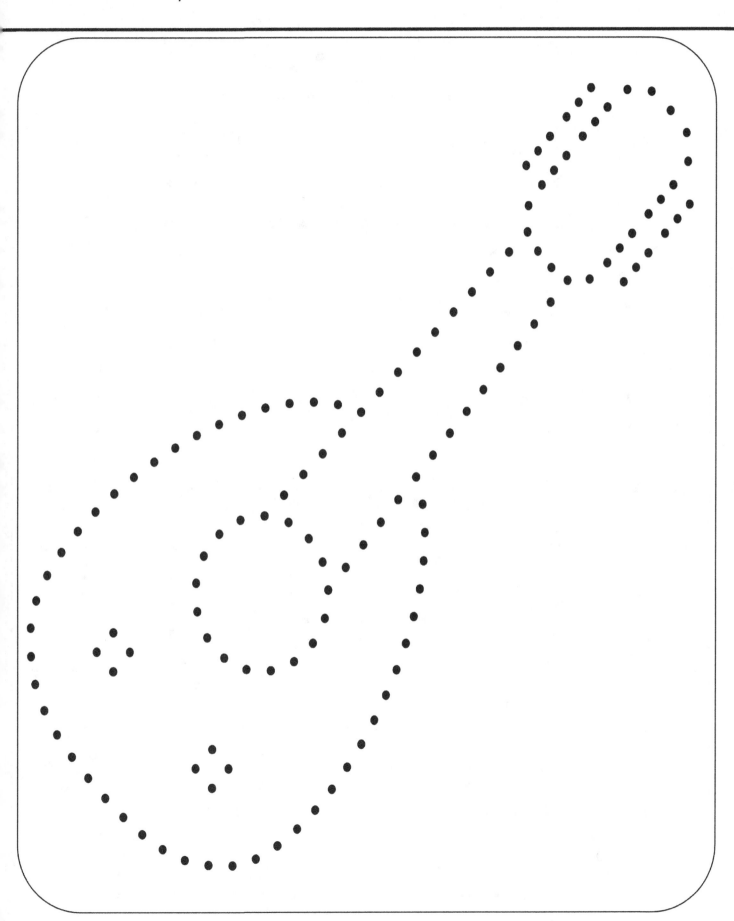

Fine motor skills practice

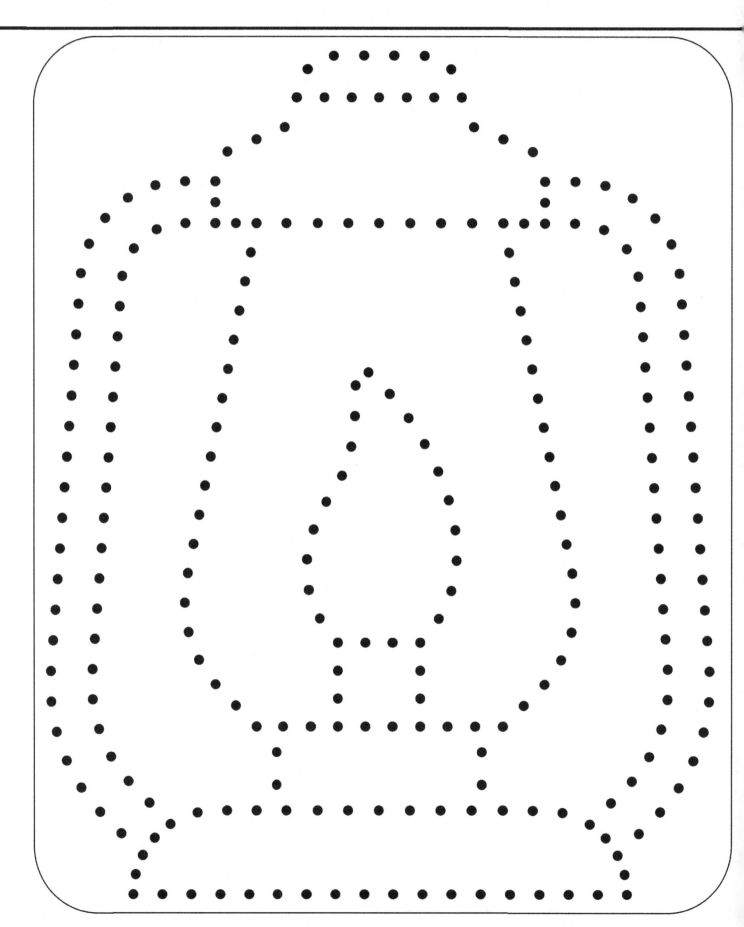

Fine motor skills practice

Fine motor skills practice

Fine motor skills practice

Fine motor skills practice

Repeat Pattern

Enhancing visual-spatial processing, attention to detail, and cognitive abilities.

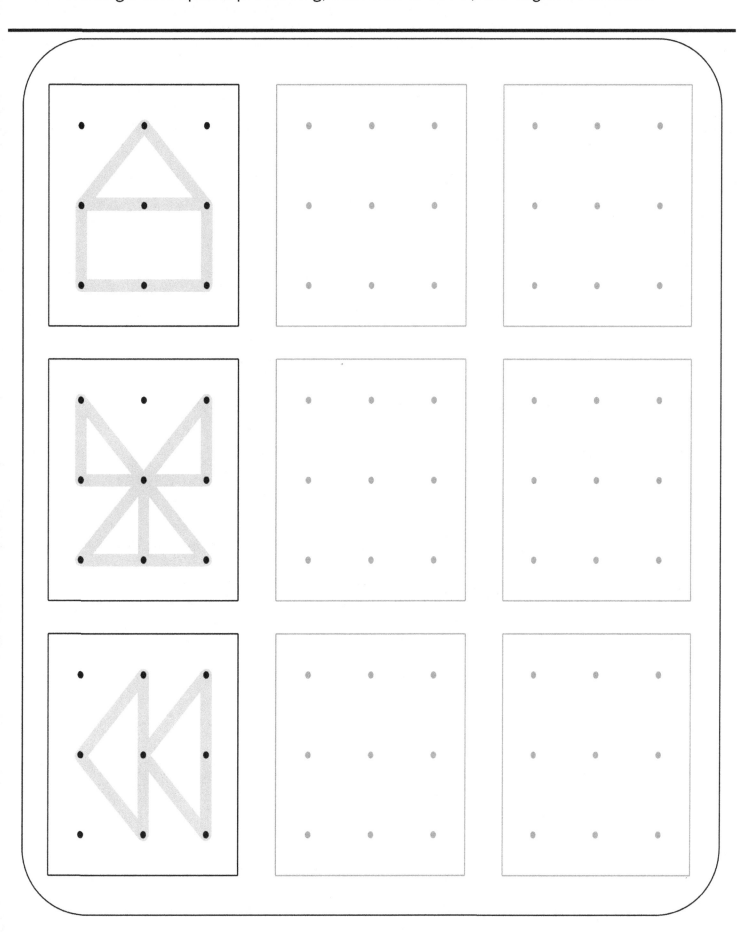

Repeat Pattern

Enhancing visual-spatial processing, attention to detail, and cognitive abilities.

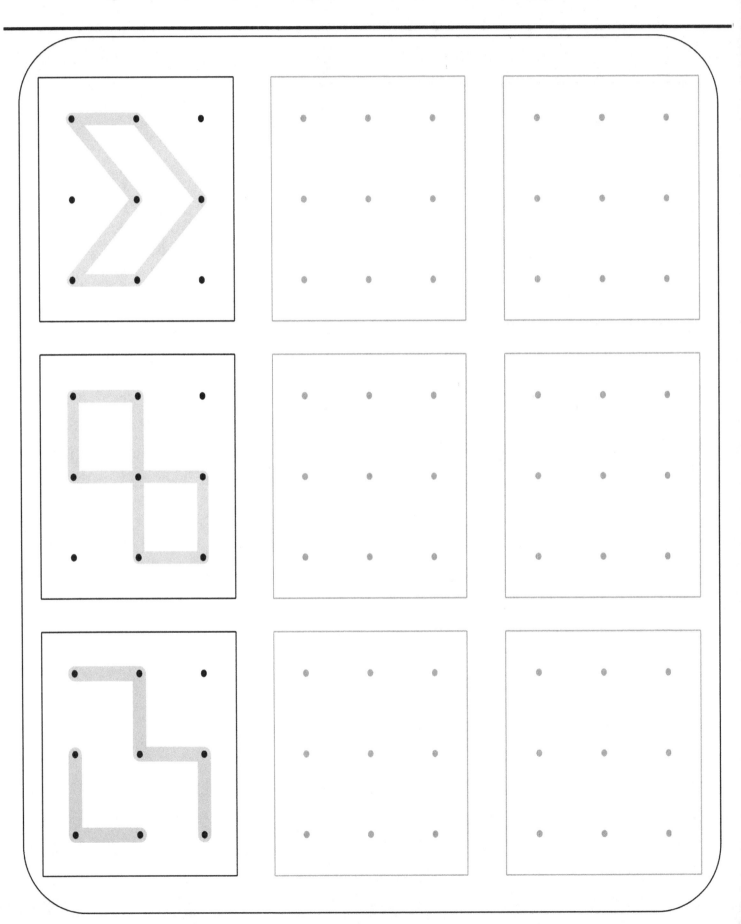

Repeat Pattern

Enhancing visual-spatial processing, attention to detail, and cognitive abilities.

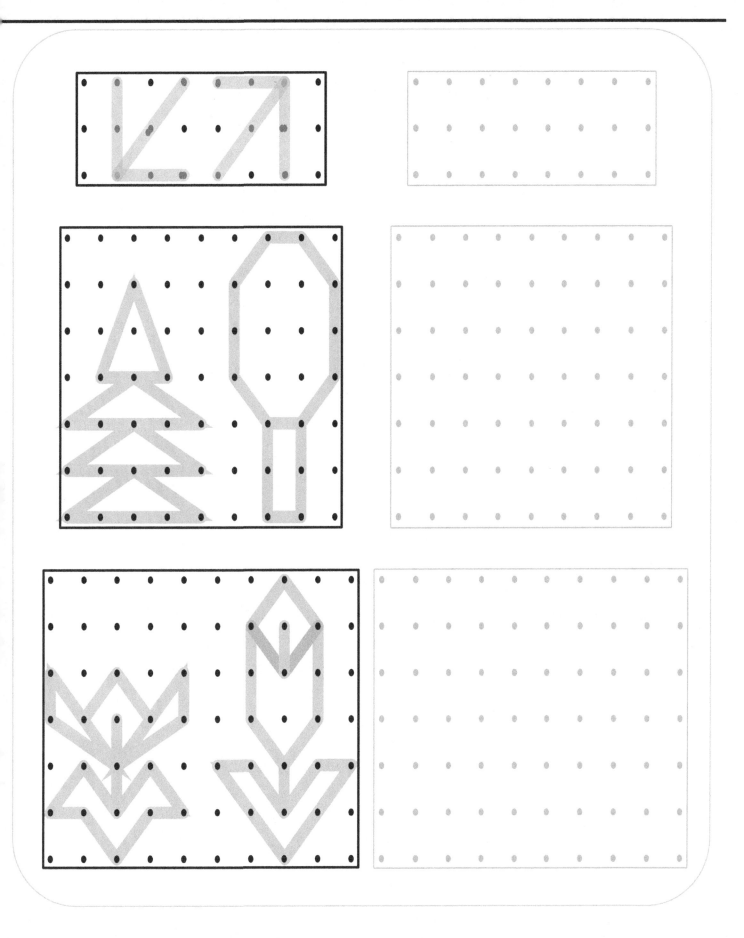

Enhancing visual-spatial processing, attention to detail, and cognitive abilities.

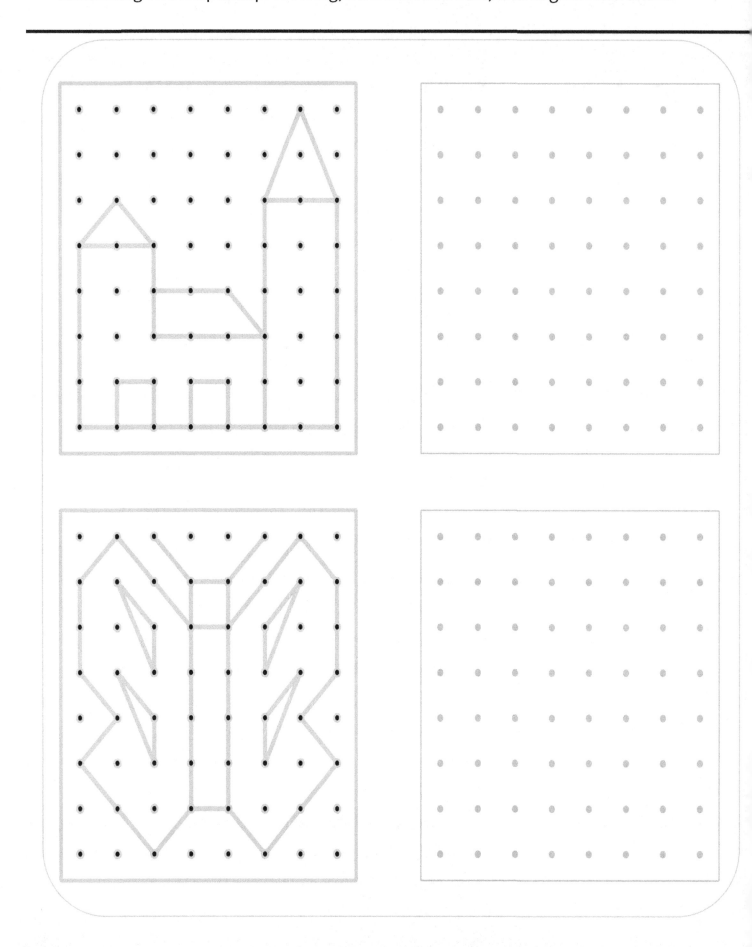

Trace Numbers

Reinforcing numerical recognition, improving fine motor skills, and promoting cognitive abilities, which collectively contribute to overall brain health and support language recovery.

Trace Numbers

Reinforcing numerical recognition, improving fine motor skills, and promoting cognitive abilities, which collectively contribute to overall brain health and support language recovery.

1 1 1 1 1 1 1 1

2 2 2 2 2 2 2 2

3 3 3 3 3 3 3 3

4 4 4 4 4 4 4 4

5 5 5 5 5 5 5 5

6 6 6 6 6 6 6 6

7 7 7 7 7 7 7 7

8 8 8 8 8 8 8 8

9 9 9 9 9 9 9 9

0 0 0 0 0 0 0 0

Trace Numbers

Tracing, counting, and identifying can help by stimulating different areas of the brain, enhancing cognitive skills, and reinforcing numerical concepts, which collectively support language recovery and overall brain health.

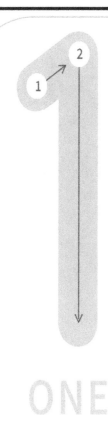

ONE

THE NUMBER ONE

Trace the number 1. Start at dot.

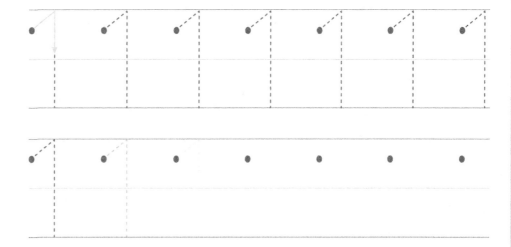

Trace the word.

Fill in all the number 1s.

Color one lemon.

Circle the box with one dot.

Circle the word 'one'.

five	six
one	nine

Count to 10 and write number 1.

 2 3 4 5 6 7 8 9 10

Trace Numbers

Tracing, counting, and identifying can help by stimulating different areas of the brain, enhancing cognitive skills, and reinforcing numerical concepts, which collectively support language recovery and overall brain health.

THE NUMBER TWO

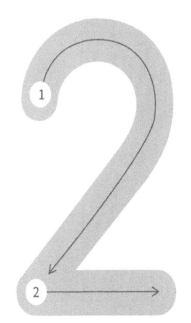

TWO

Trace the number 2. Start at dot.

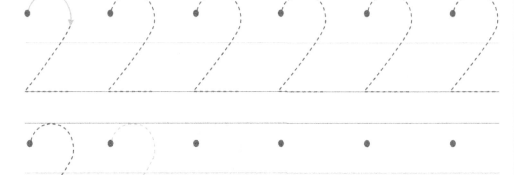

Trace the word.

two two two two

Fill in all the number 2s.

Color two pears.

Circle the dice with two dots.

Circle the word 'two'.

one	four
three	two

Count to 10 and write number 2.

 1 3 4 5 6 7 8 9 10

Trace Numbers

Tracing, counting, and identifying can help by stimulating different areas of the brain, enhancing cognitive skills, and reinforcing numerical concepts, which collectively support language recovery and overall brain health.

THE NUMBER THREE

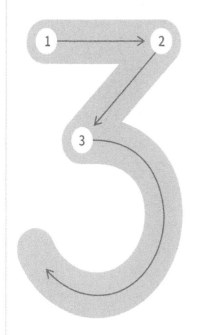

THREE

Trace the number 3. Start at dot.

Trace the word.

three   three   three

Fill in all the number 3s.

Count to 10 and write number 3.

Color three strawberries.

Circle the dice with three dots.

Circle the word 'three'.

five	two
four	three

 1   2   3   4   5   6   7   8   9   10

Trace Numbers

Tracing, counting, and identifying can help by stimulating different areas of the brain, enhancing cognitive skills, and reinforcing numerical concepts, which collectively support language recovery and overall brain health.

THE NUMBER FOUR

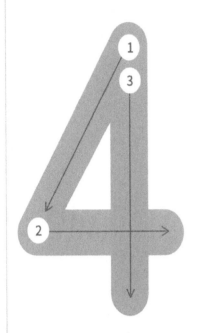

FOUR

Trace the number 4. Start at dot.

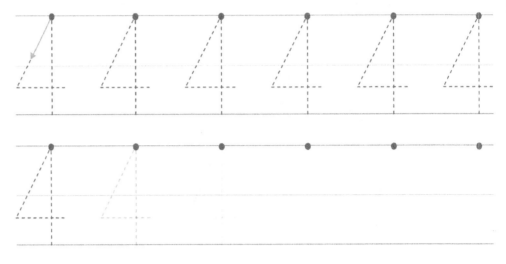

Trace the word.

four four four four

Fill in all the number 4s.

Color four pencils.

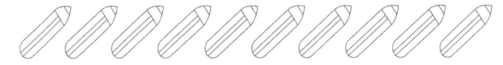

Circle the dice with four dots.

Circle the word 'four'.

one	seven
four	five

Count to 10 and write number 4.

1 2 3 ☐ 5 6 7 8 9 10

Tracing, counting, and identifying can help by stimulating different areas of the brain, enhancing cognitive skills, and reinforcing numerical concepts, which collectively support language recovery and overall brain health.

THE NUMBER FIVE

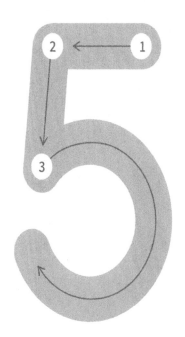

FIVE

Trace the number 5. Start at dot.

Trace the word.

five five five five

Fill in all the number 5s.

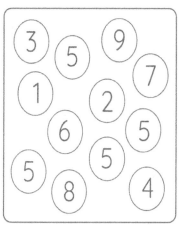

Color five oranges.

Circle the dice with five dots.

Circle the word 'five'.

two	nine
six	five

Count to 10 and write number 5.

1 2 3 4 6 7 8 9 10

Tracing, counting, and identifying can help by stimulating different areas of the brain, enhancing cognitive skills, and reinforcing numerical concepts, which collectively support language recovery and overall brain health.

THE NUMBER SIX

SIX

Trace the number 6. Start at dot.

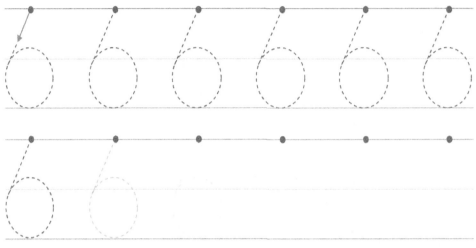

Trace the word.

six six six six six

Fill in all the number 6s.

Color six watermelon slices.

Circle the dice with six dots.

Circle the word 'six'.

one	eight
six	seven

Count to 10 and write number 6.

1 2 3 4 5 ⬚ 7 8 9 10

Tracing, counting, and identifying can help by stimulating different areas of the brain, enhancing cognitive skills, and reinforcing numerical concepts, which collectively support language recovery and overall brain health.

THE NUMBER SEVEN

Trace the number 7. Start at dot.

Trace the word.

SEVEN

seven seven seven

Fill in all the number 7s.

Color seven flowers.

Circle the dice with seven dots.

Circle the word 'seven'.

two	six
nine	seven

Count to 10 and write number 7.

1   2   3   4   5   6   [ ]   8   9   10

Trace Numbers

Tracing, counting, and identifying can help by stimulating different areas of the brain, enhancing cognitive skills, and reinforcing numerical concepts, which collectively support language recovery and overall brain health.

THE NUMBER EIGHT

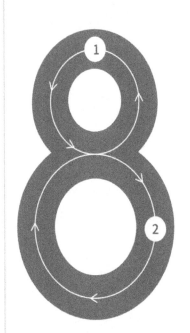

Trace the number 8. Start at dot.

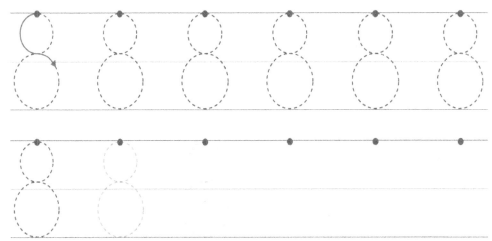

Trace the word.

eight eight eight

EIGHT

Fill in all the number 8s.

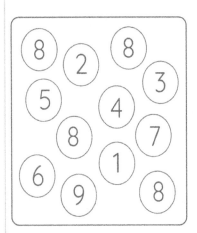

Color eight moons.

Circle the dice with eight dots.

Circle the word 'eight'.

eight	seven
three	one

Count to 10 and write number 8.

1 2 3 4 5 6 7   9 10

Trace Numbers

Tracing, counting, and identifying can help by stimulating different areas of the brain, enhancing cognitive skills, and reinforcing numerical concepts, which collectively support language recovery and overall brain health.

THE NUMBER NINE

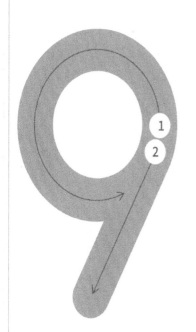

NINE

Trace the number 9. Start at dot.

Trace the word.

nine nine nine nine

Fill in all the number 9s.

Color nine rockets.

Circle the dice with nine dots.

Circle the word 'nine'.

five	nine
two	three

Count to 10 and write number 9.

1 2 3 4 5 6 7 8 [ ] 10

Tracing, counting, and identifying can help by stimulating different areas of the brain, enhancing cognitive skills, and reinforcing numerical concepts, which collectively support language recovery and overall brain health.

THE NUMBER TEN

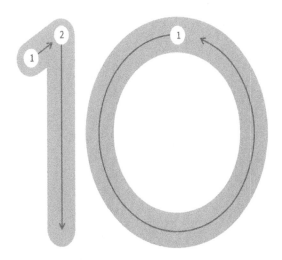

TEN

NUMBER 10 IS MADE UP OF
TWO NUMBERS: ONE AND ZERO

Trace the number 10. Start at dot.

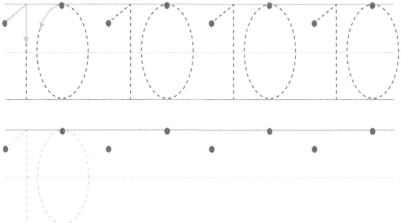

Trace the word.

ten ten ten ten

Fill in all the number 10s.

Color ten stars.

Circle the dice with ten dots.

Circle the word 'ten'.

two	ten
three	five

Count to 10 and write number 10.

1 2 3 4 5 6 7 8 9

Reinforcing numerical recognition, improving fine motor skills, and promoting cognitive abilities, which collectively contribute to overall brain health and support language recovery.

Trace Numbers

Reinforcing numerical recognition, improving fine motor skills, and promoting cognitive abilities, which collectively contribute to overall brain health and support language recovery.

Trace Numbers

Reinforcing numerical recognition, improving fine motor skills, and promoting cognitive abilities, which collectively contribute to overall brain health and support language recovery.

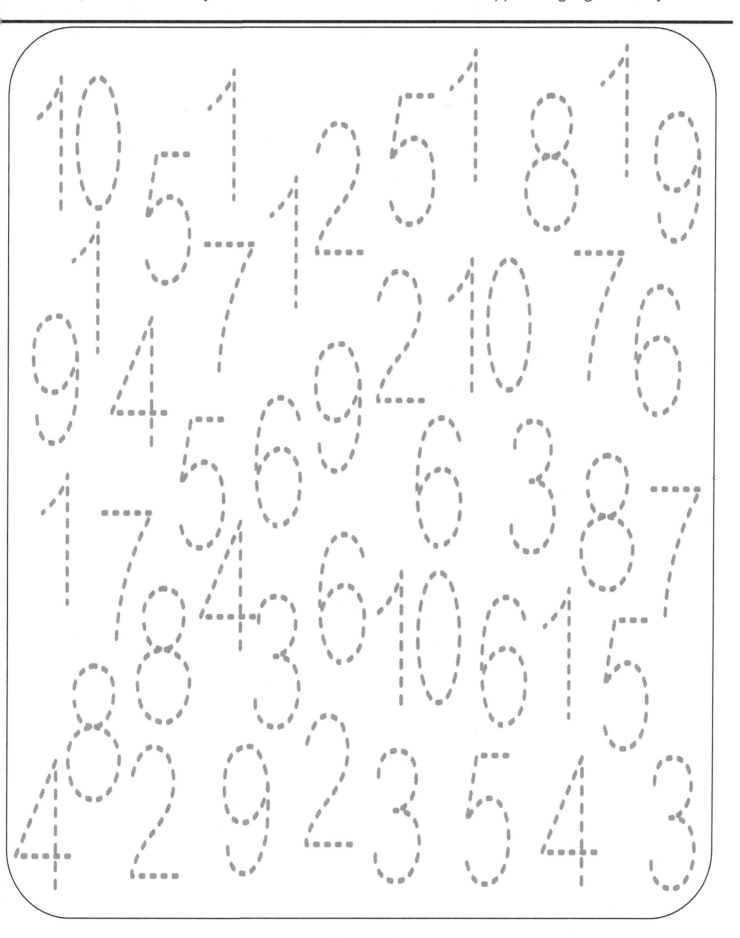

Reinforcing numerical recognition, improving fine motor skills, and promoting cognitive abilities, which collectively contribute to overall brain health and support language recovery.

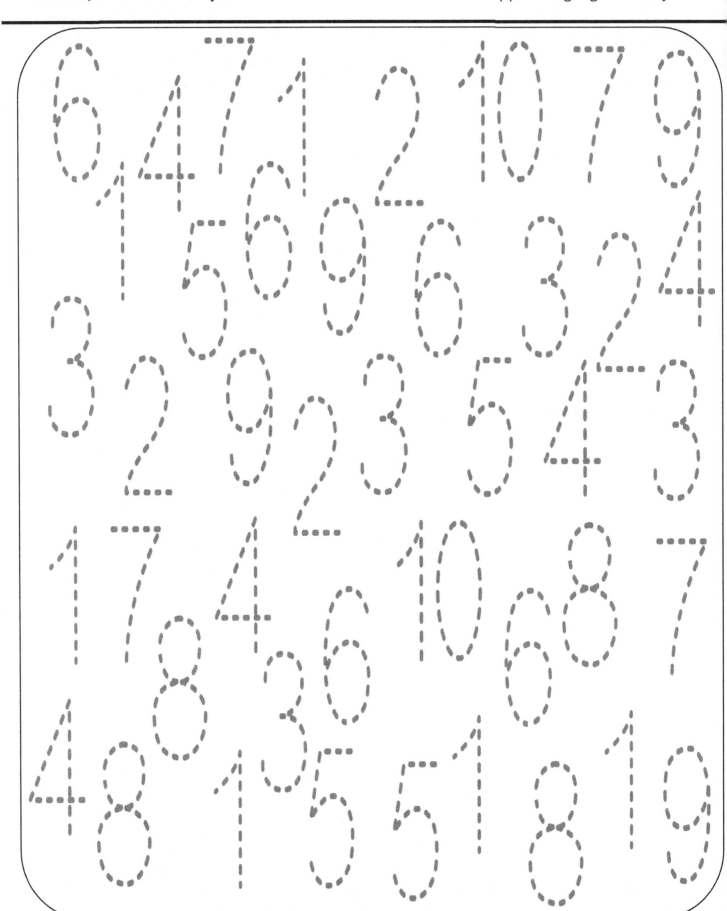

Trace Numbers

Reinforcing numerical recognition, improving fine motor skills, and promoting cognitive abilities, which collectively contribute to overall brain health and support language recovery.

Trace Numbers

Reinforcing numerical recognition, improving fine motor skills, and promoting cognitive abilities, which collectively contribute to overall brain health and support language recovery.

Tracing

Fine motor skills practice

Fine motor skills practice

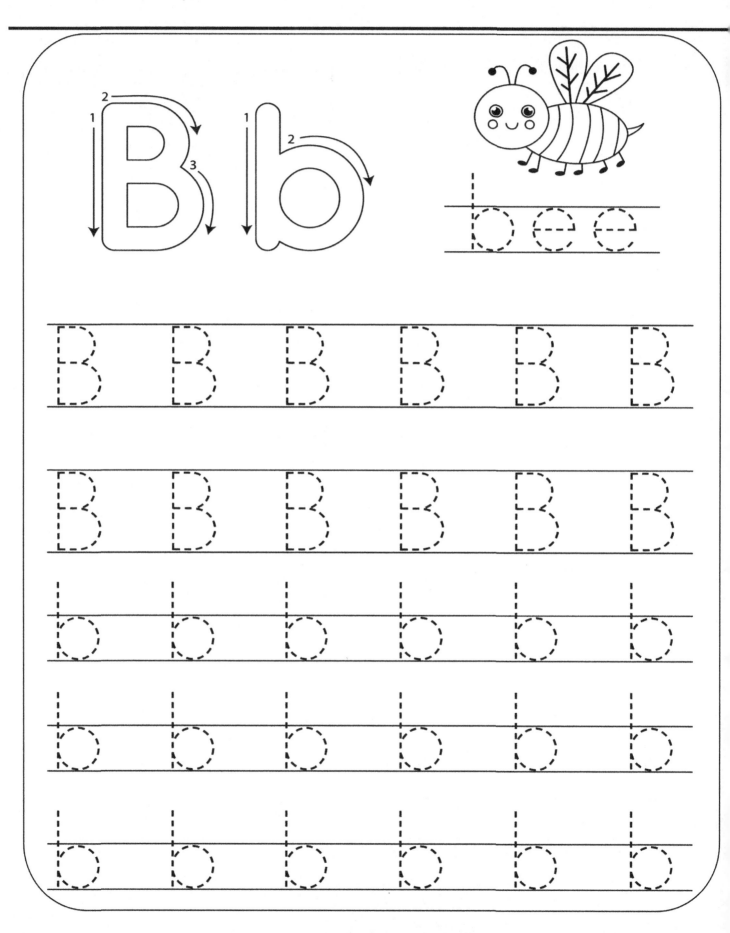

Fine motor skills practice

crab

Fine motor skills practice

Fine motor skills practice

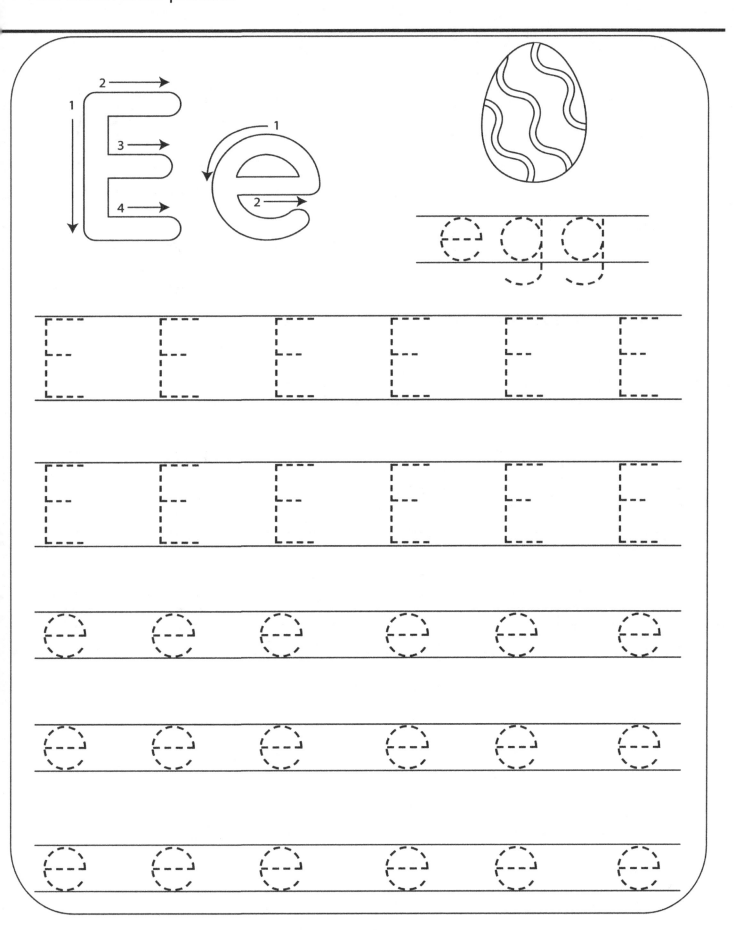

Fine motor skills practice

Tracing

Fine motor skills practice

Tracing

Fine motor skills practice

Fine motor skills practice

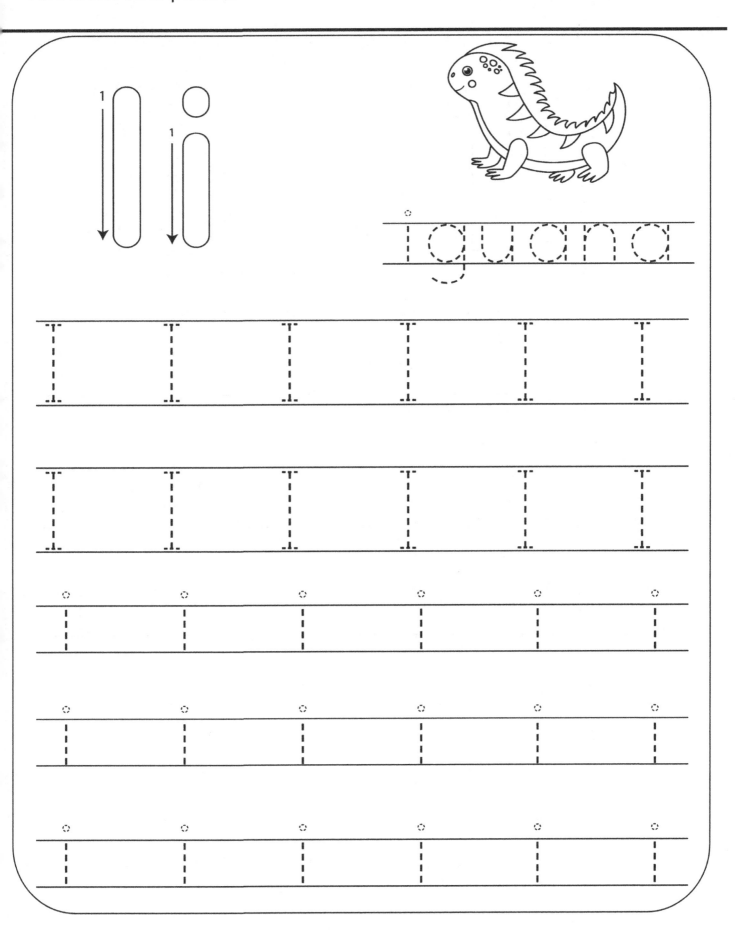

iguana

Fine motor skills practice

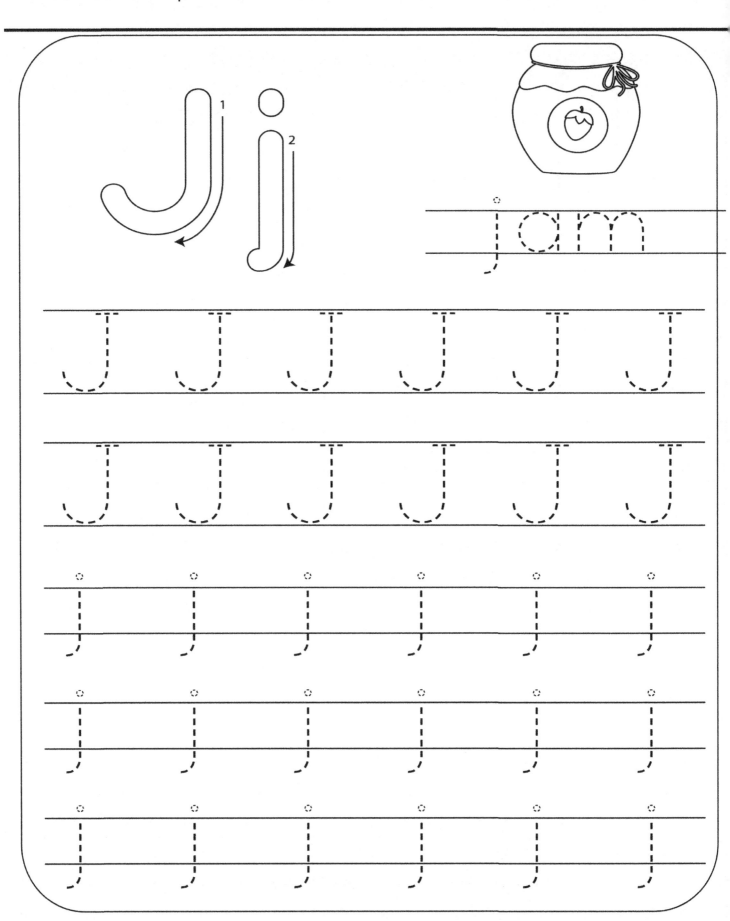

Fine motor skills practice

koala

Tracing
Fine motor skills practice

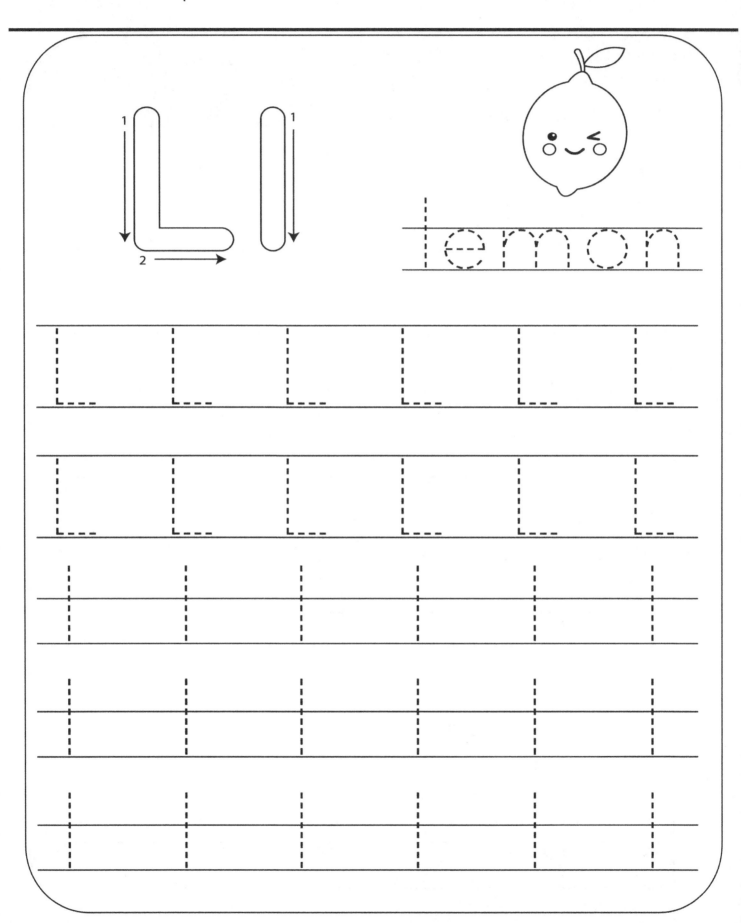

Fine motor skills practice

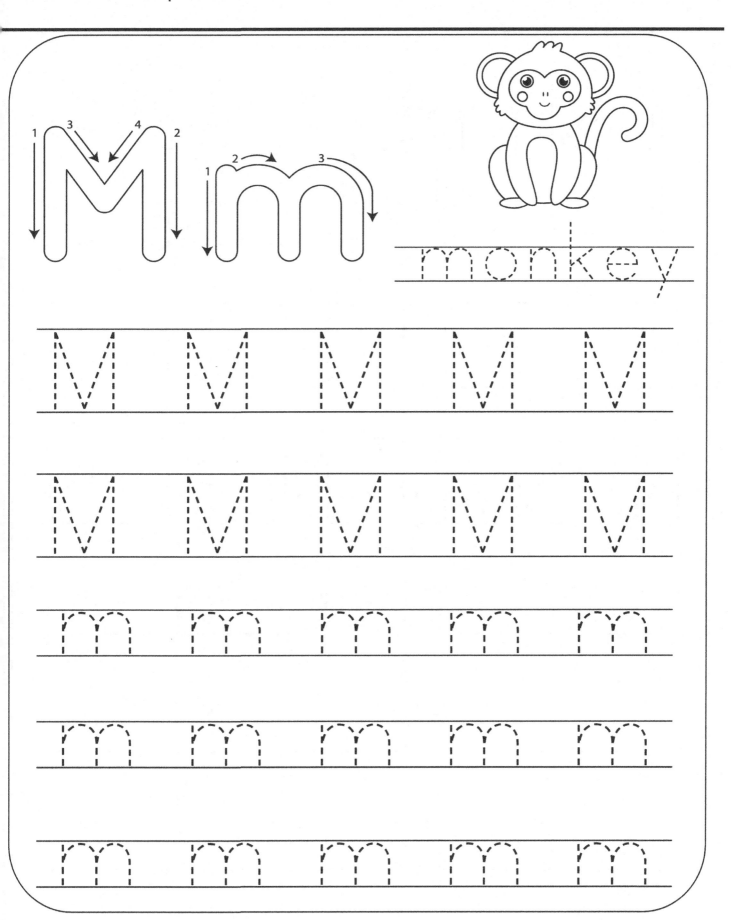

monkey

Tracing

Fine motor skills practice

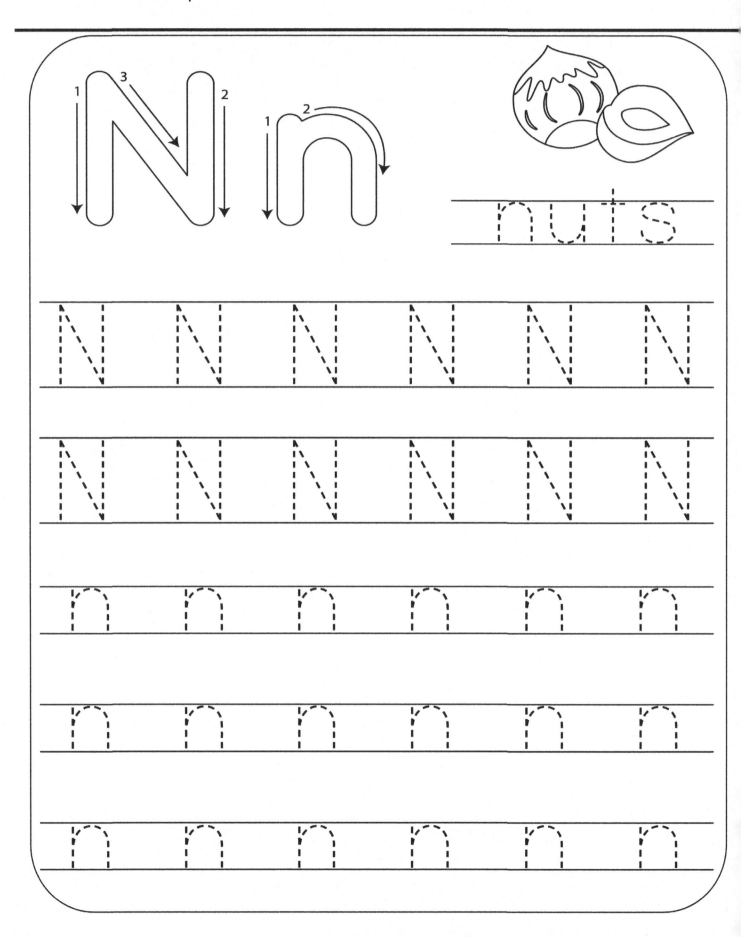

Fine motor skills practice

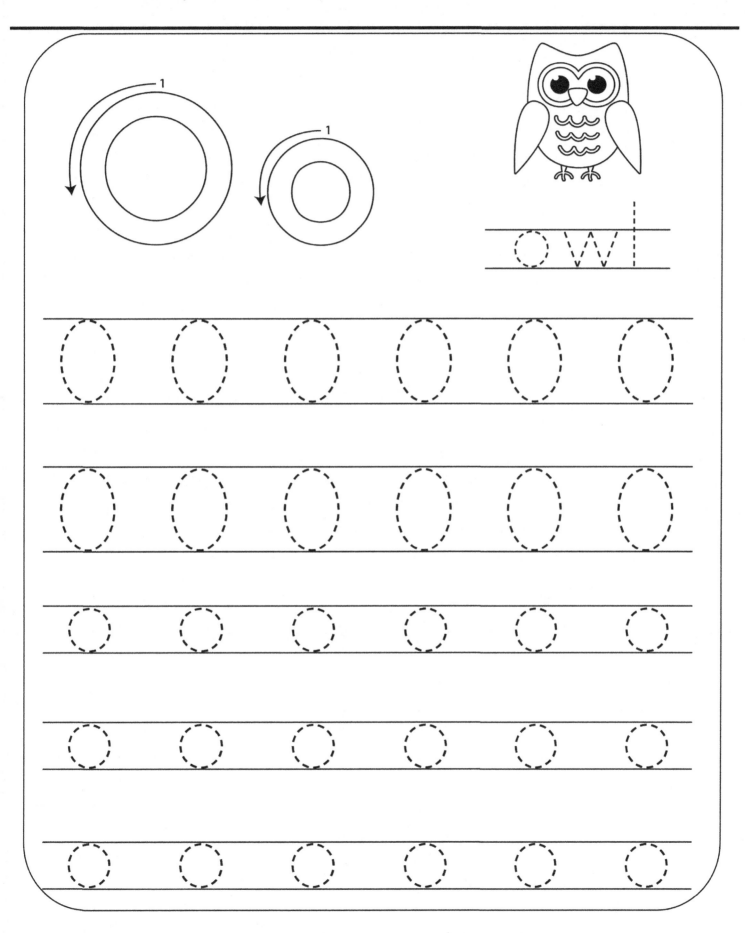

Tracing

Fine motor skills practice

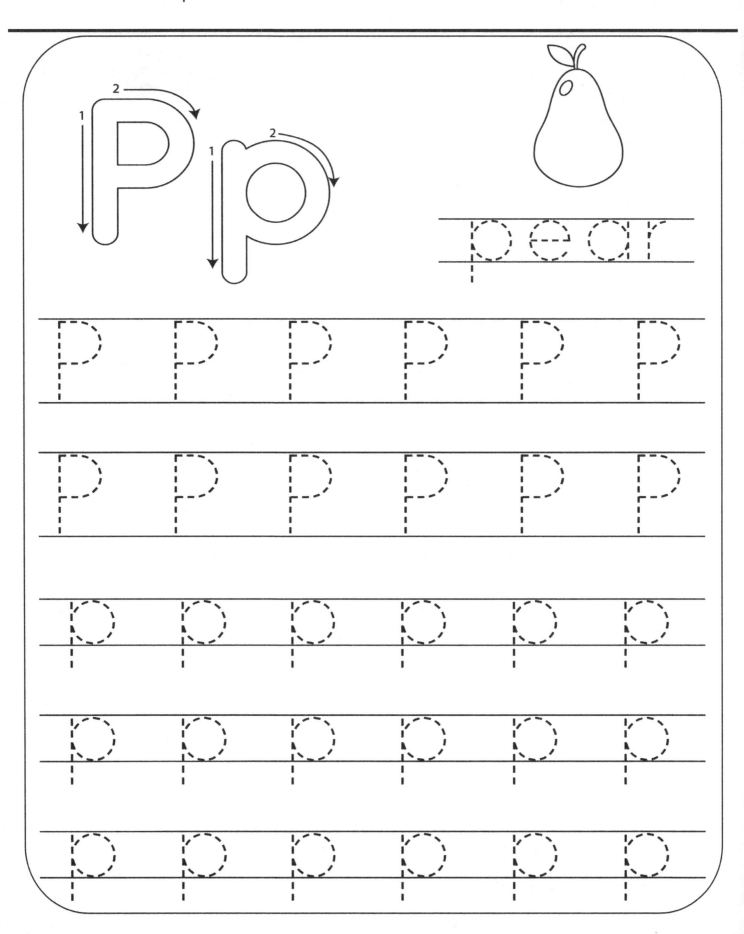

Fine motor skills practice

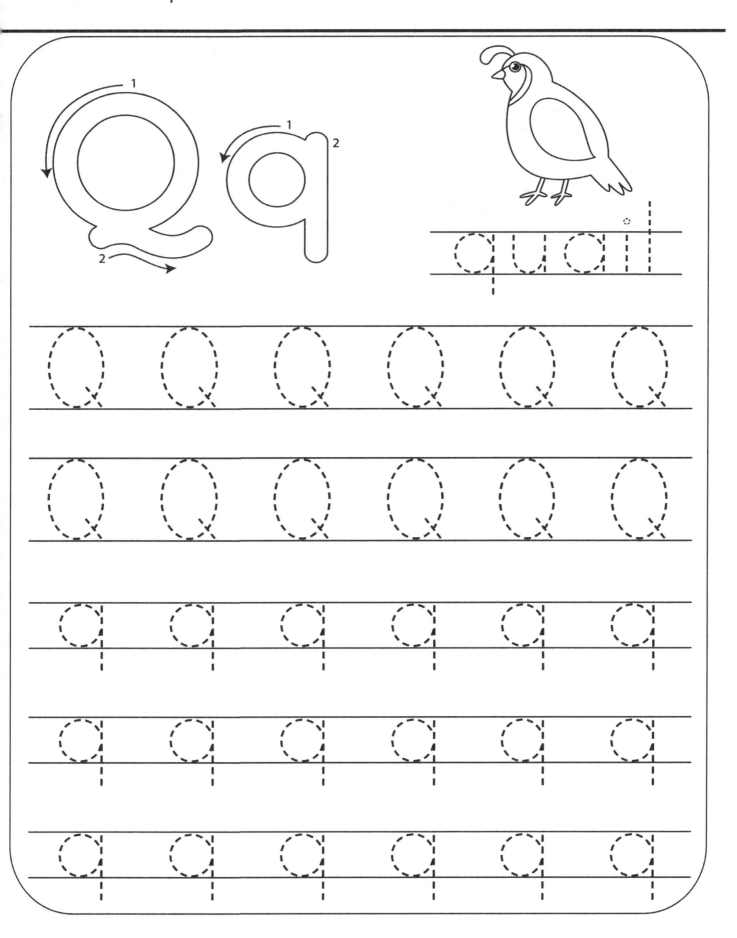

Fine motor skills practice

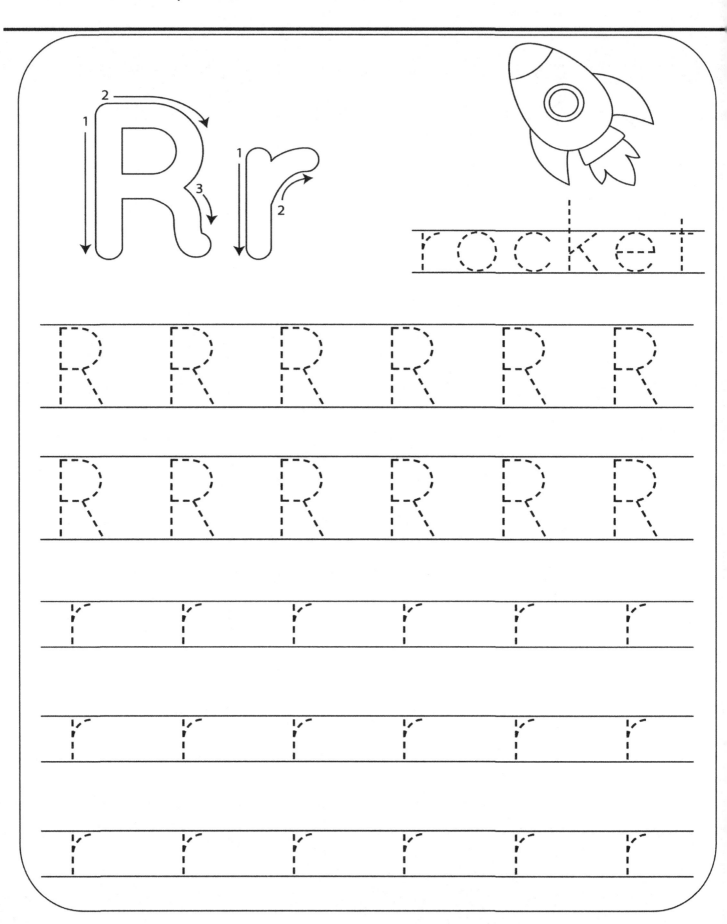

rocket

Fine motor skills practice

Tracing

Fine motor skills practice

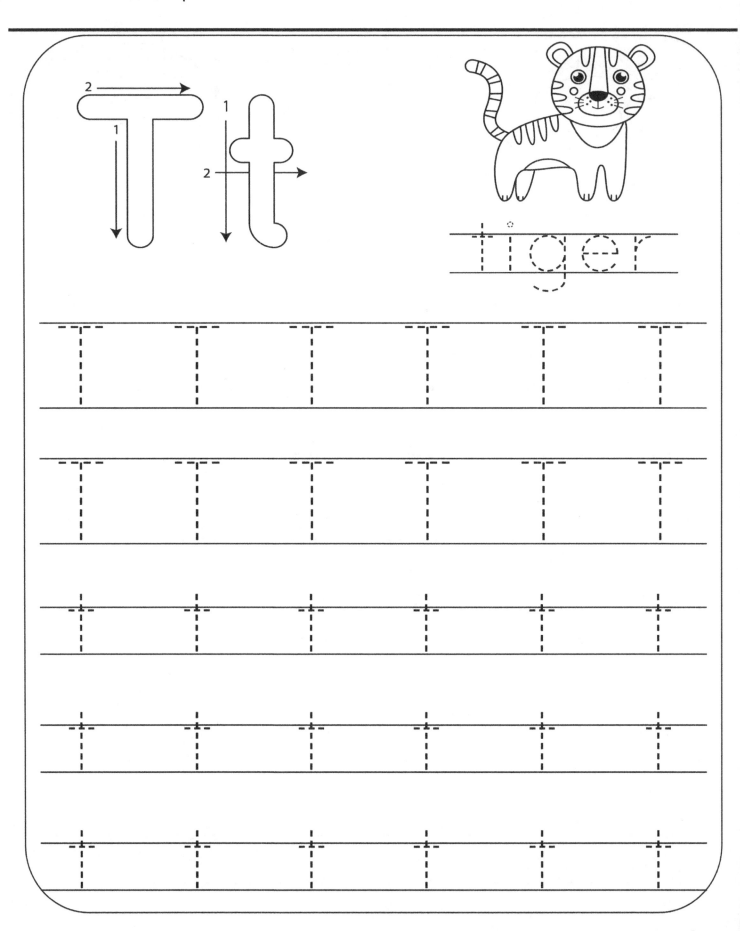

Fine motor skills practice

Fine motor skills practice

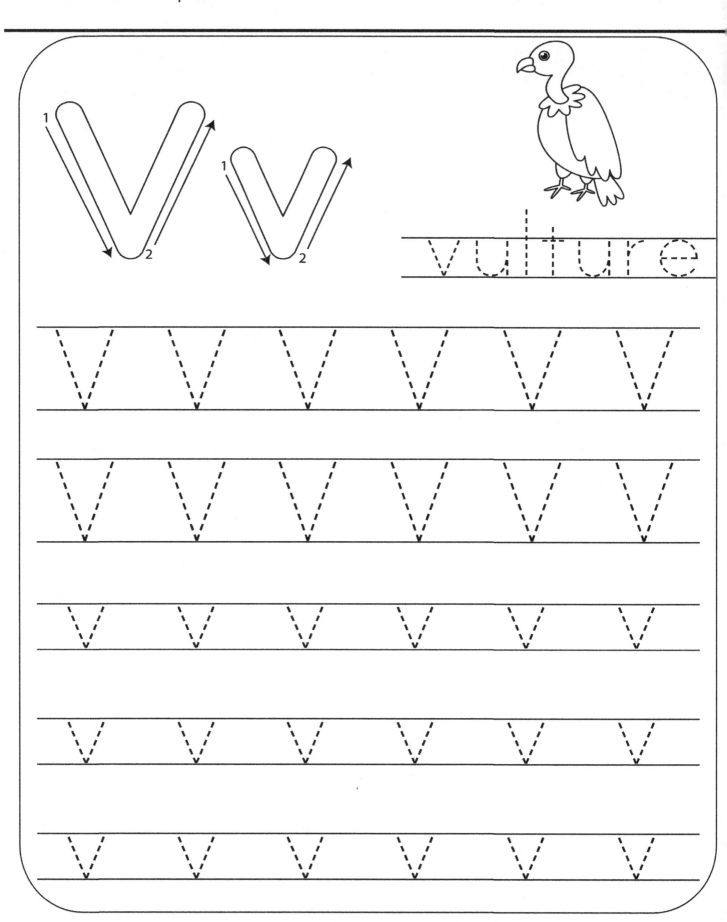

vulture

Fine motor skills practice

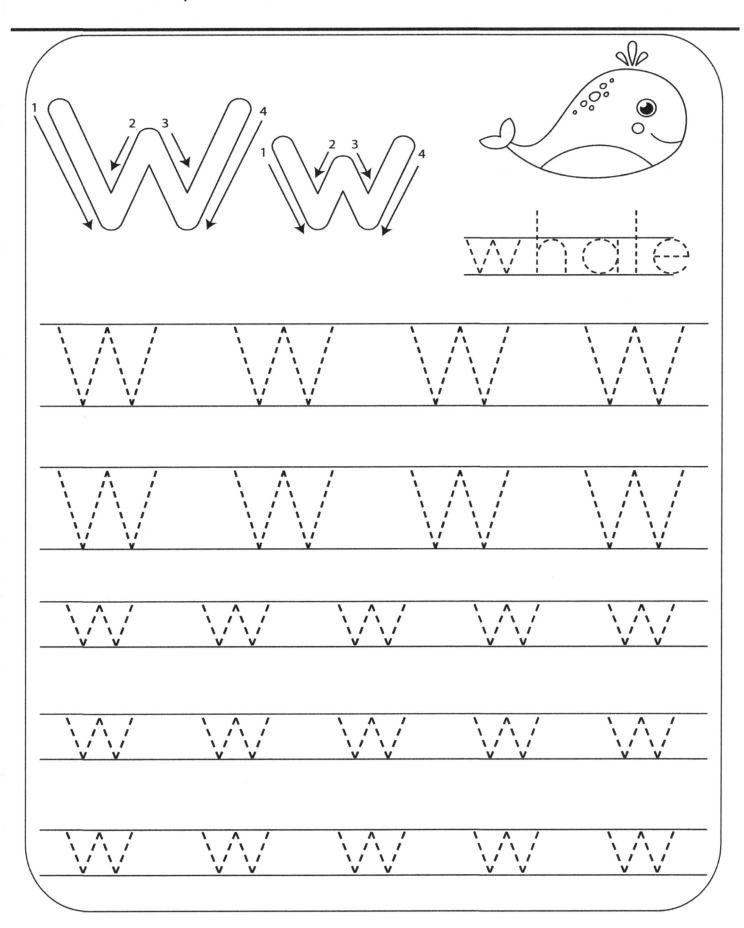

Tracing

Fine motor skills practice

x ray fish

Fine motor skills practice

yak

Tracing

Fine motor skills practice

zebra

Trace and write days of the week.

Monday

Monday   Monday

Monday   Monday

Monday   Monday

Monday   Monday

Monday   Monday

Monday   Monday

Trace and write days of the week.

Tuesday   Tuesday

Tuesday   Tuesday

Tuesday   Tuesday

Tuesday   Tuesday

Tuesday   Tuesday

Tuesday   Tuesday

Trace and write days of the week.

Wednesday

Wednesday Wednesday

Wednesday Wednesday

Wednesday Wednesday

Wednesday Wednesday

Wednesday Wednesday

Wednesday Wednesday

Trace and write days of the week.

Thursday

Thursday Thursday

Thursday Thursday

Thursday Thursday

Thursday Thursday

Thursday Thursday

Thursday Thursday

Trace and write days of the week.

Friday   Friday   Friday

Friday   Friday   Friday

Friday   Friday   Friday

Friday   Friday   Friday

Friday   Friday   Friday

Friday   Friday   Friday

Trace and write days of the week.

Saturday

Saturday   Saturday

Saturday   Saturday

Saturday   Saturday

Saturday   Saturday

Saturday   Saturday

Saturday   Saturday

Days of the Week
Trace and write days of the week.

Sunday

Sunday   Sunday

Sunday   Sunday

Sunday   Sunday

Sunday   Sunday

Sunday   Sunday

Sunday   Sunday

Copy the Trail

How This Helps

This exercise can be beneficial for you as a person with aphasia because it helps improve your visual-spatial skills, hand-eye coordination, and attention to detail. By focusing on tracing the pattern and following the specific path while connecting the dots, you'll be engaging and reinforcing the neural connections related to spatial awareness, concentration, and sequential planning.

Practicing these skills can lead to improvements in your overall cognitive abilities, which may, in turn, contribute to your language recovery and enhance your communication skills. Remember to be patient with yourself and take your time, as repetition and practice are essential for strengthening these cognitive skills.

Instructions

1) Look at the two columns of dots on the page. One column will have the dots connected, forming a pattern or path.
2) Carefully observe the connected dots in the left column, noting the direction and order in which they are connected.
3) Shift your focus to the other column, which contains the same arrangement of dots but without the connections.
4) Using a pen or pencil, start connecting the dots in the right column, following the same pattern and path as shown in the left column.
Pay close attention to the direction and order of the connections, ensuring that your path in the right column matches the example in the left column.
5) Once you have completed the path in the right column, compare it with the left column to check for accuracy and make any necessary adjustments.
6) Remember to take your time and concentrate on the details of the path.

The key to successfully completing this exercise is to focus on accurately replicating the pattern and direction of the connected dots.

Copy the Trail

Copy the trail by connecting the dots.

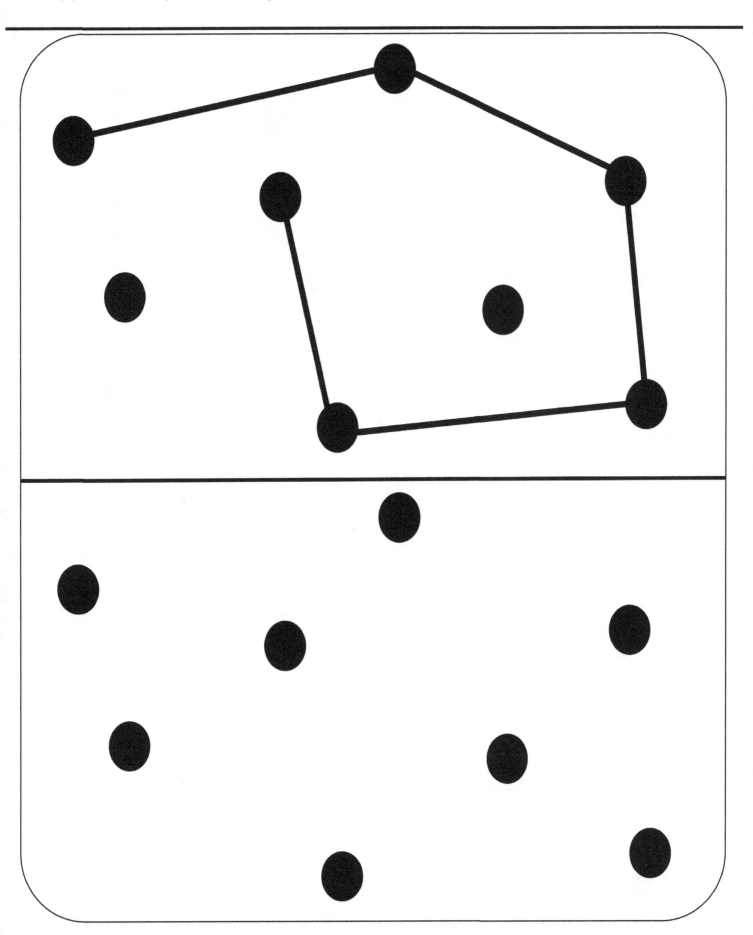

Copy the Trail

Copy the trail by connecting the dots.

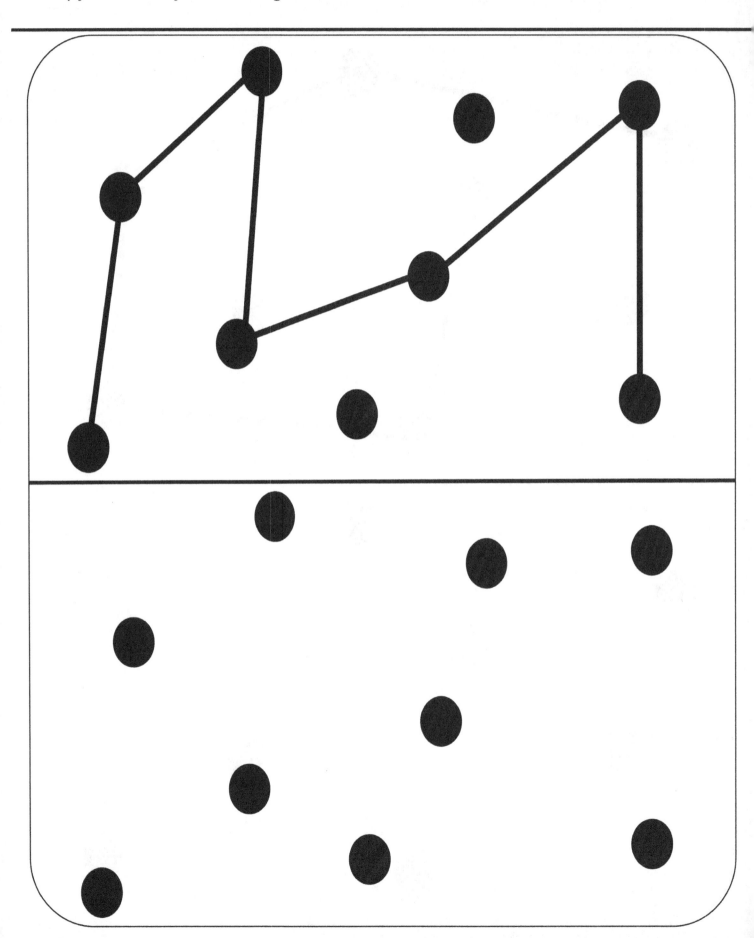

Copy the route by connecting the dots.

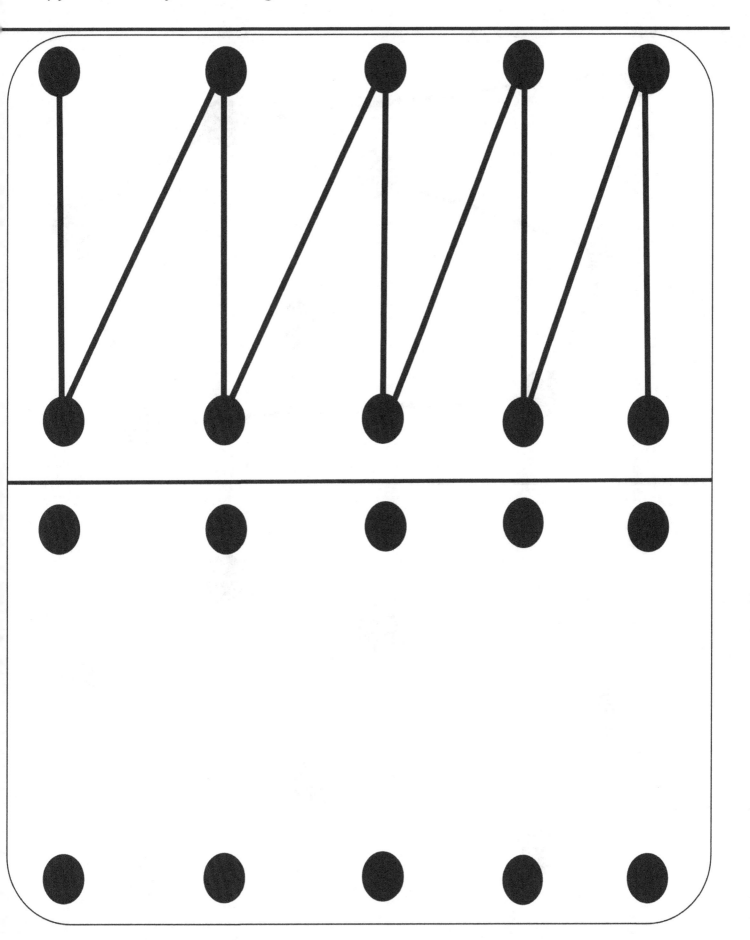

Copy the route by connecting the dots.

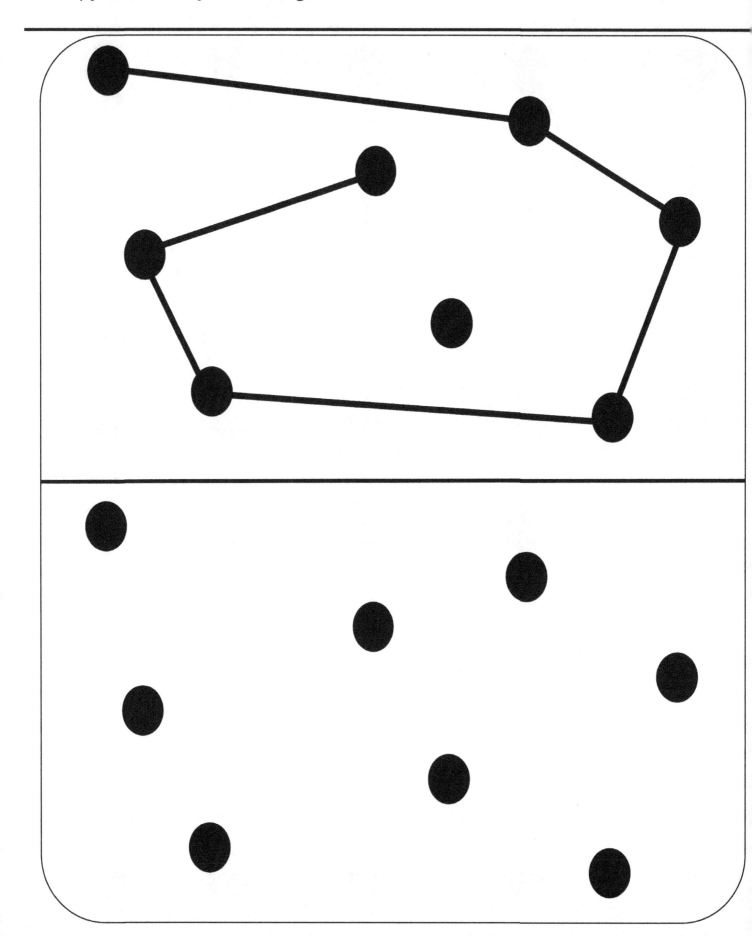

Copy the route by connecting the dots.

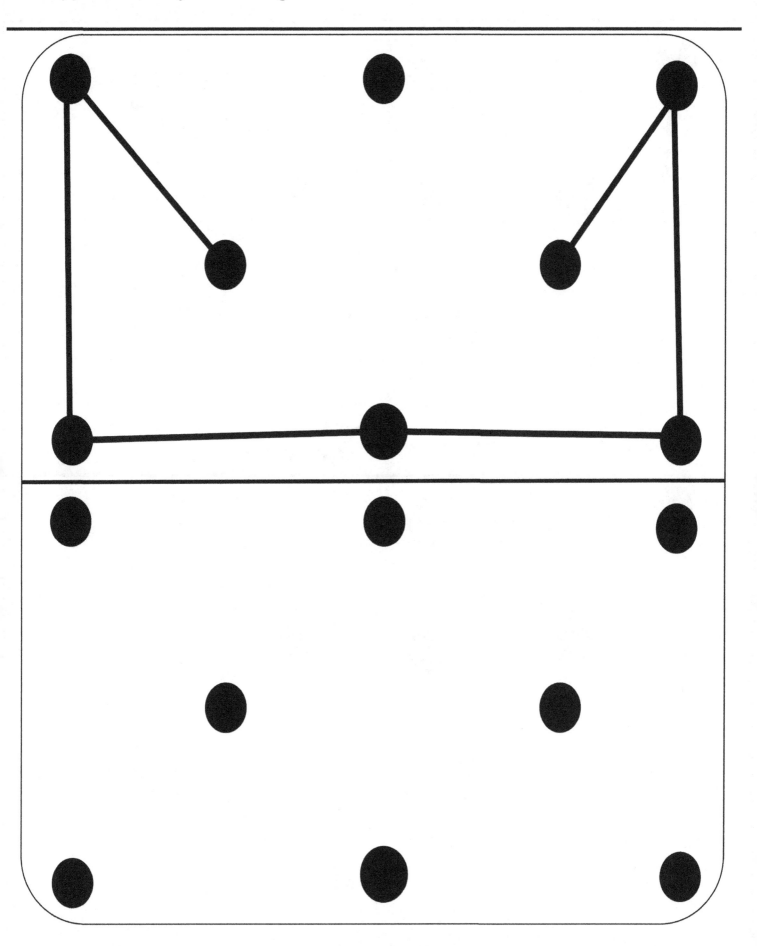

Copy the route by connecting the dots.

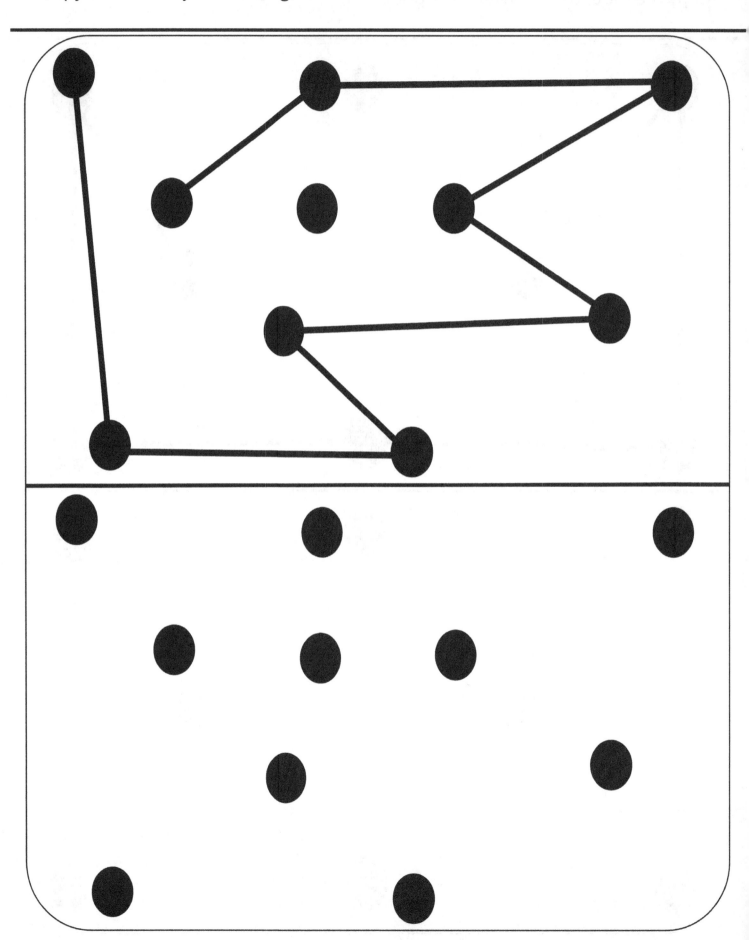

Copy the route by connecting the dots.

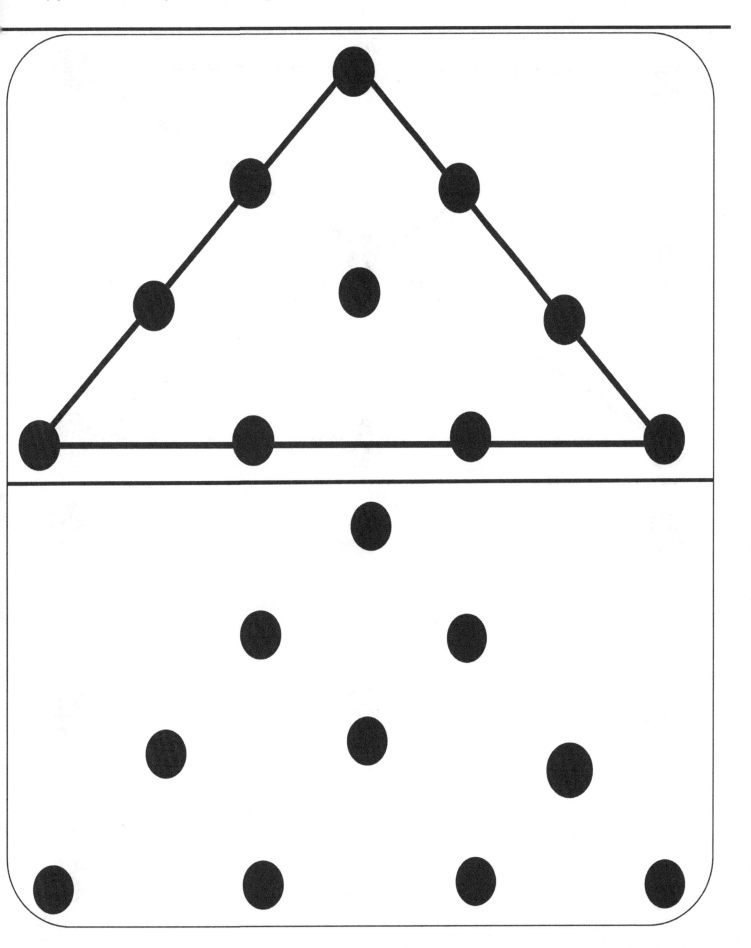

Copy the Trail

Copy the route by connecting the dots.

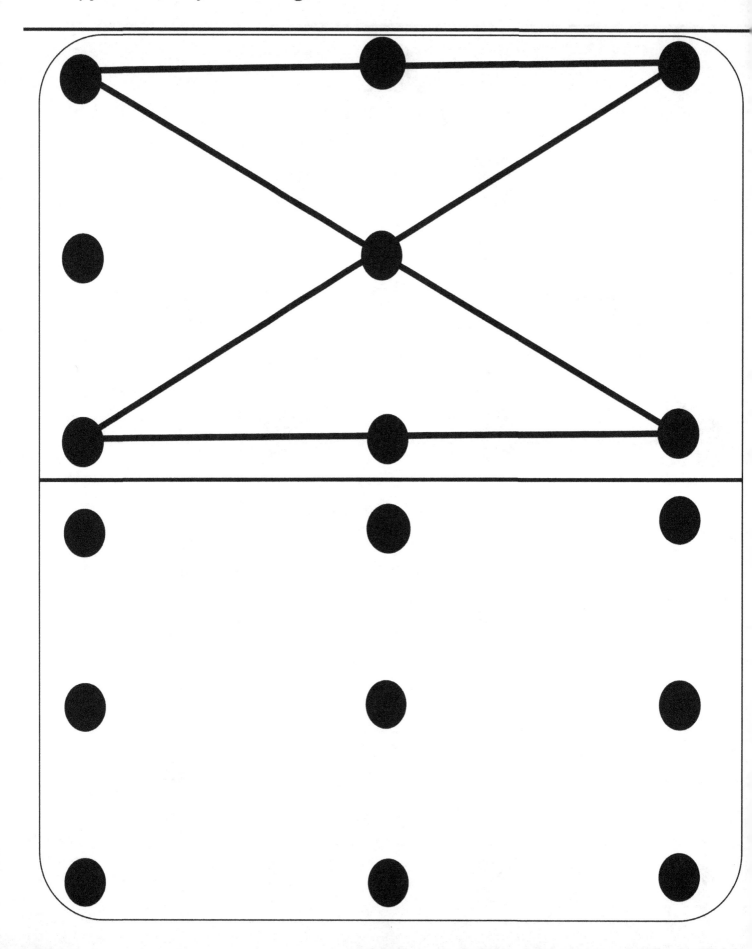

Copy the Trail

Copy the route by connecting the dots.

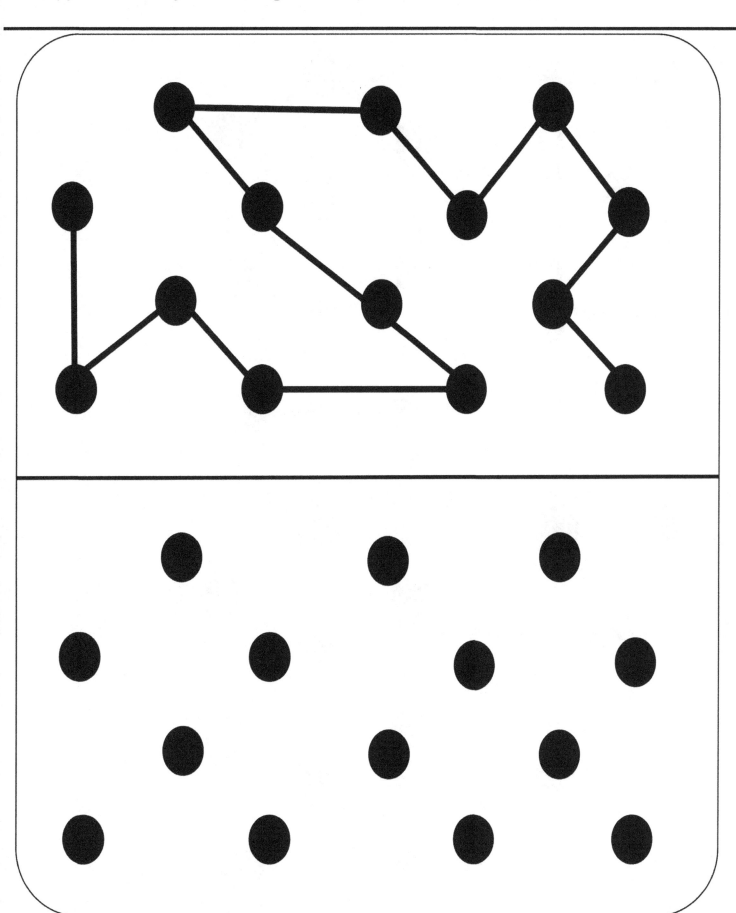

Copy the Trail

Copy the route by connecting the dots.

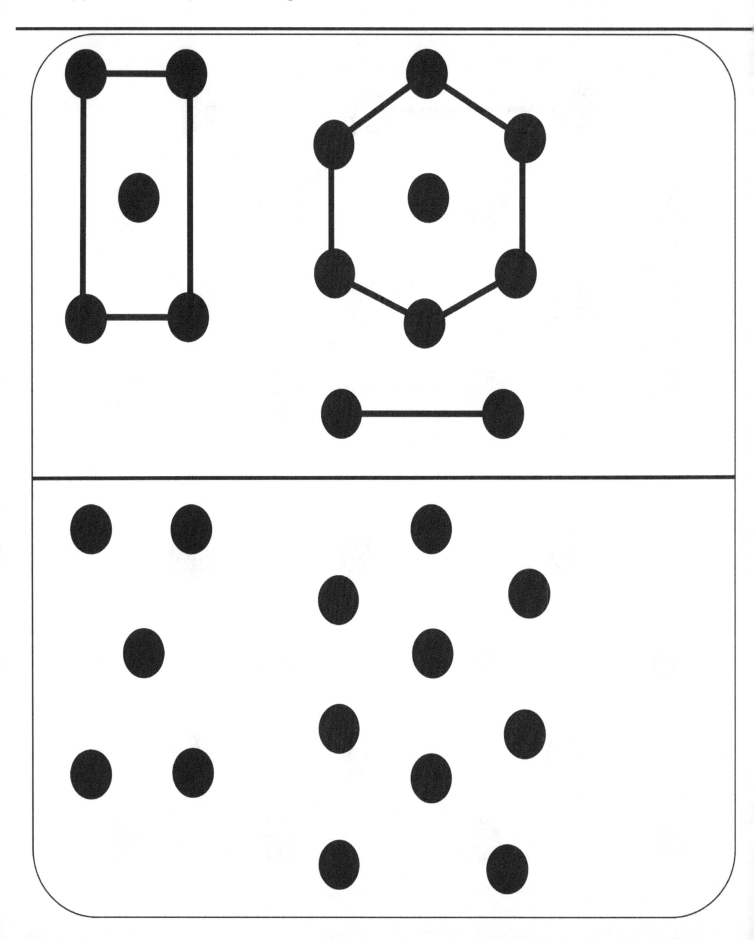

Copy the Trail

Copy the route by connecting the dots.

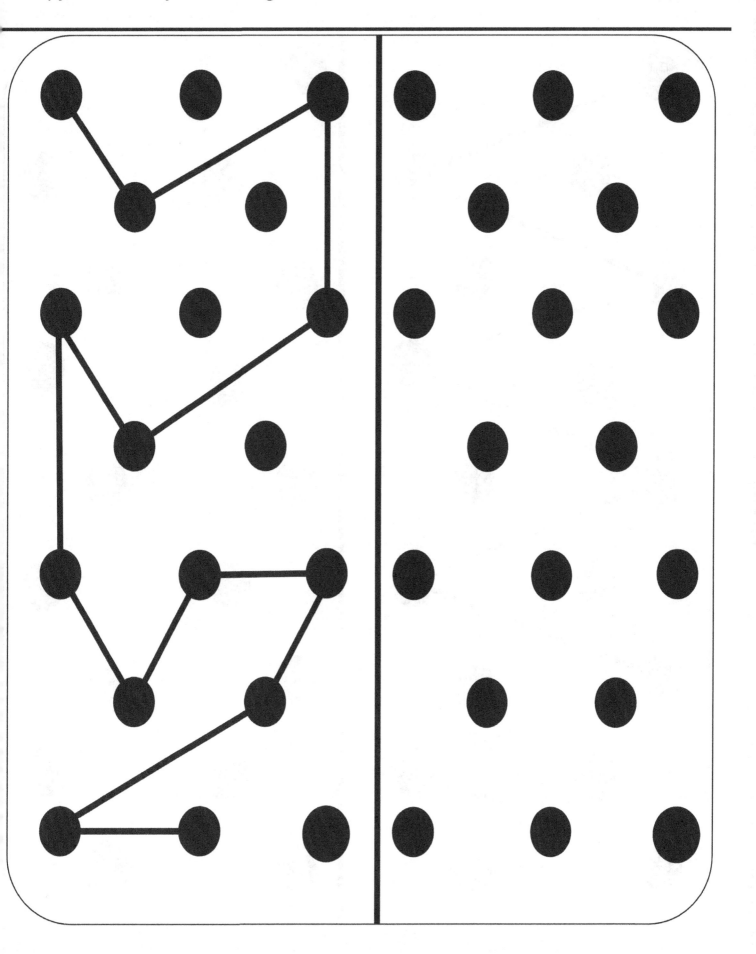

Copy the route by connecting the dots.

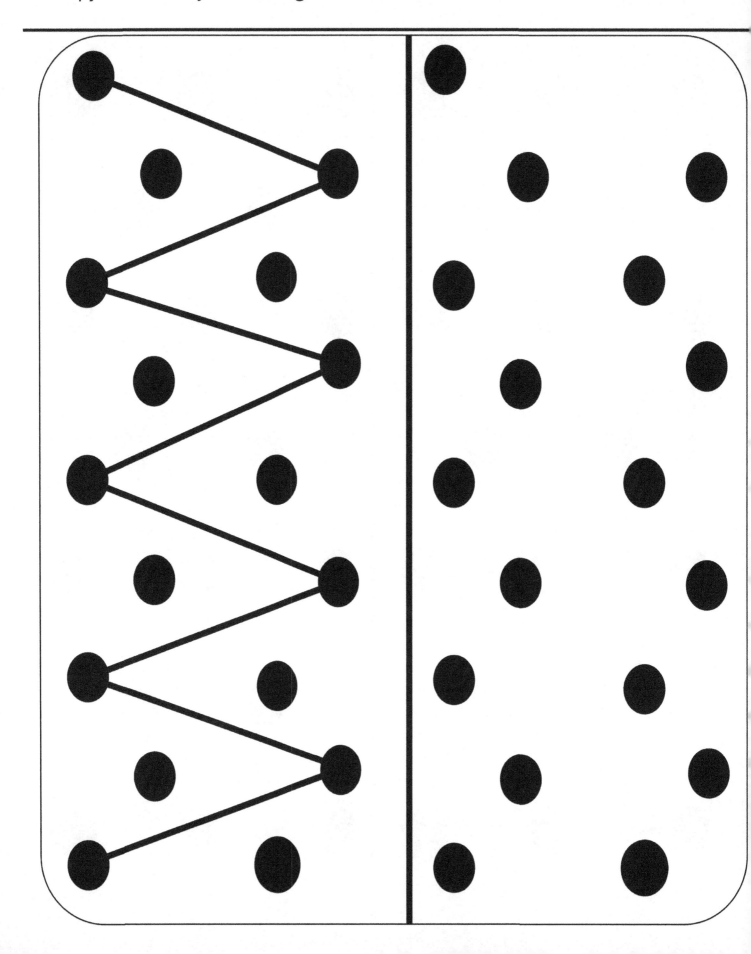

Copy the Trail

Copy the route by connecting the dots.

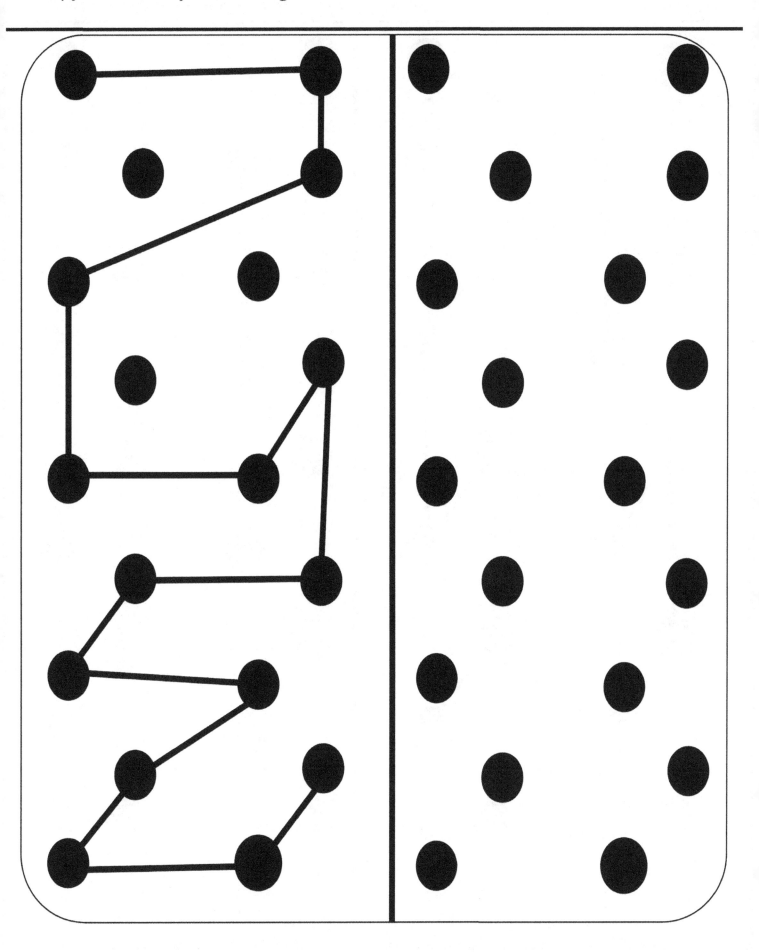

Copy the Trail

Copy the route by connecting the dots.

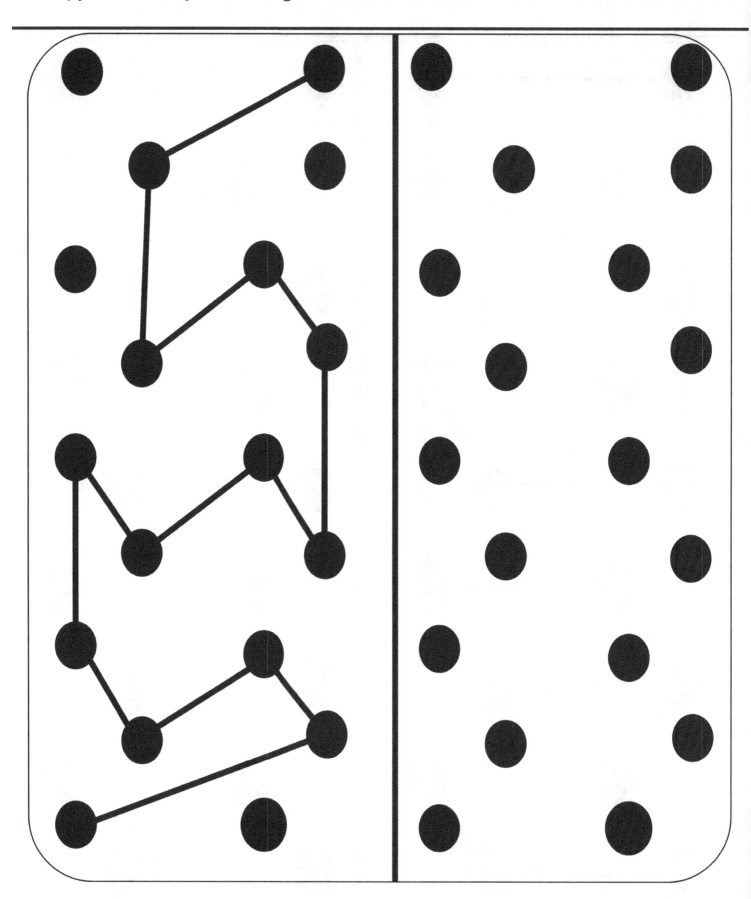

Copy the Trail

Copy the route by connecting the dots.

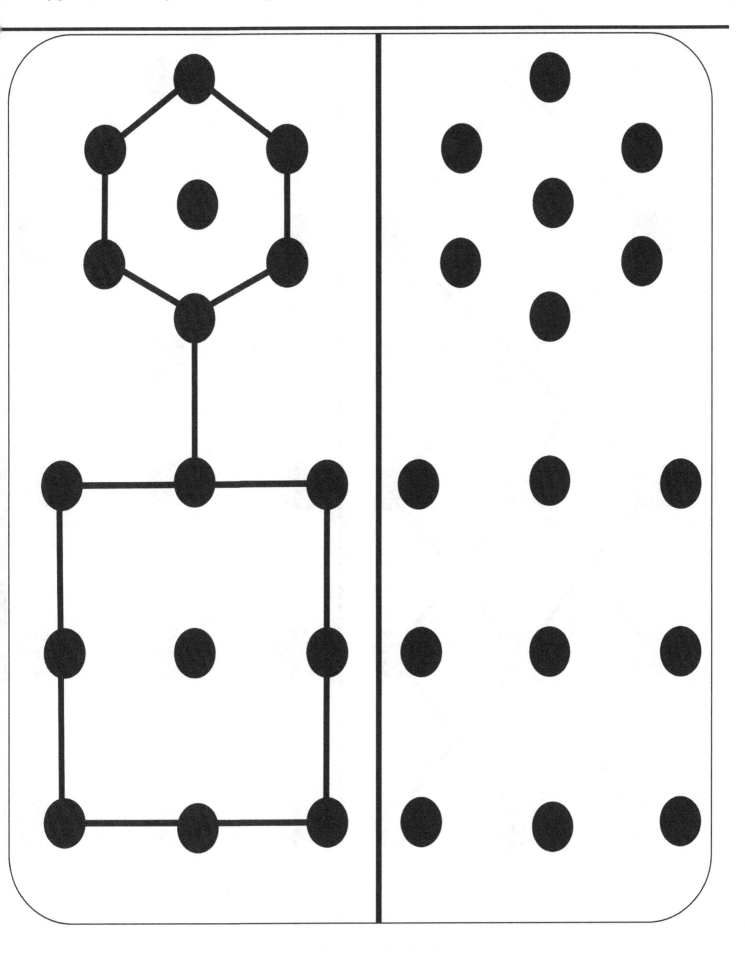

Copy the Trail

Copy the route by connecting the dots.

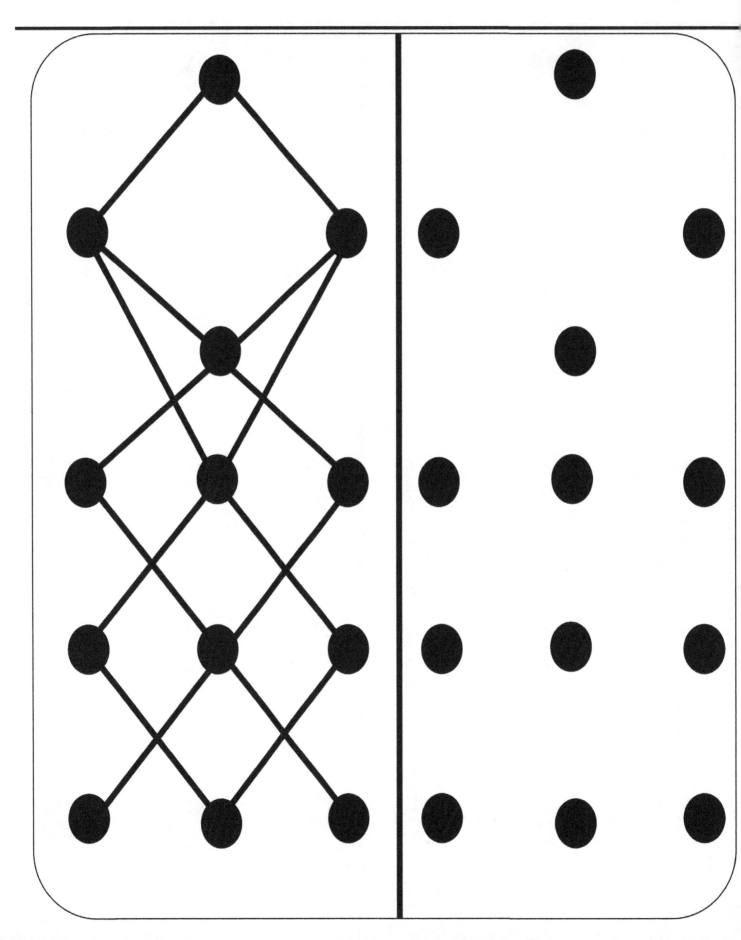

Copy the Trail

Copy the route by connecting the dots.

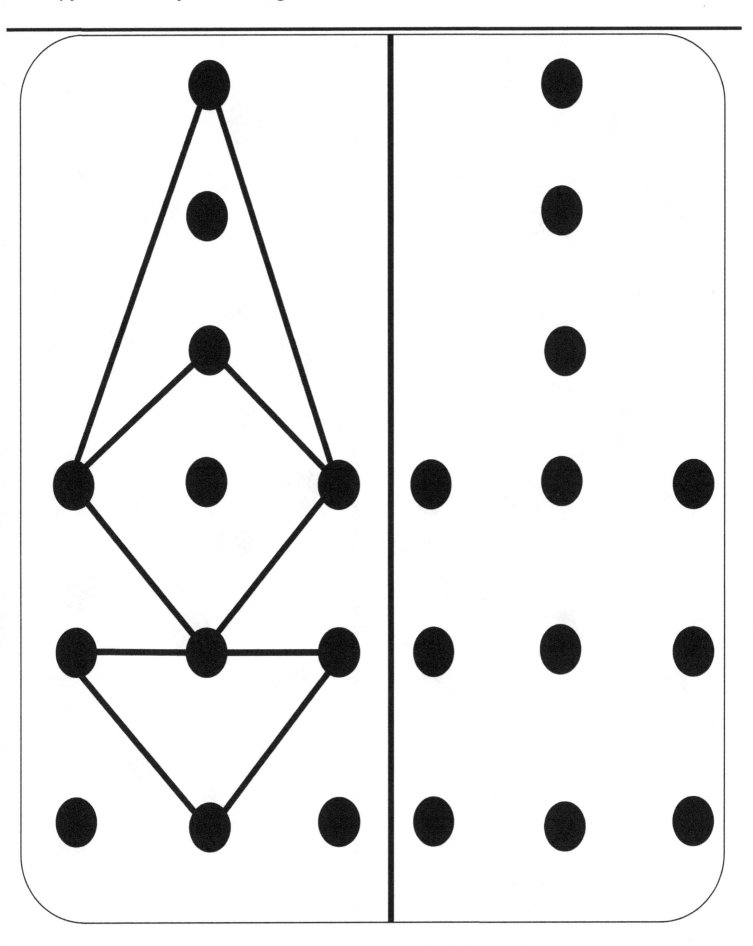

Copy the route by connecting the dots.

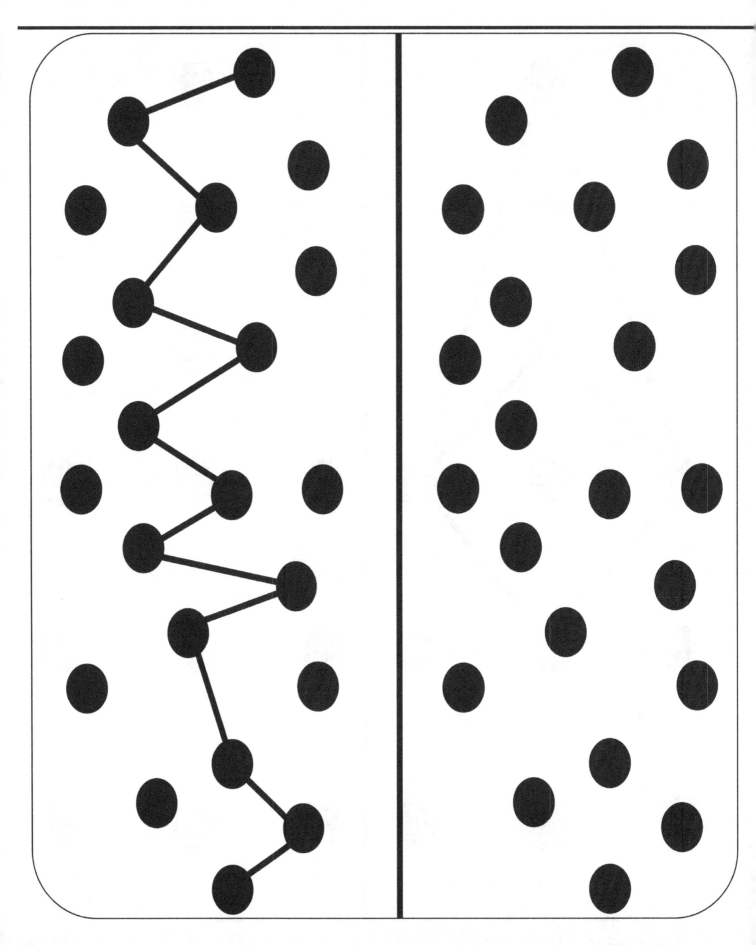

Copy the route by connecting the dots.

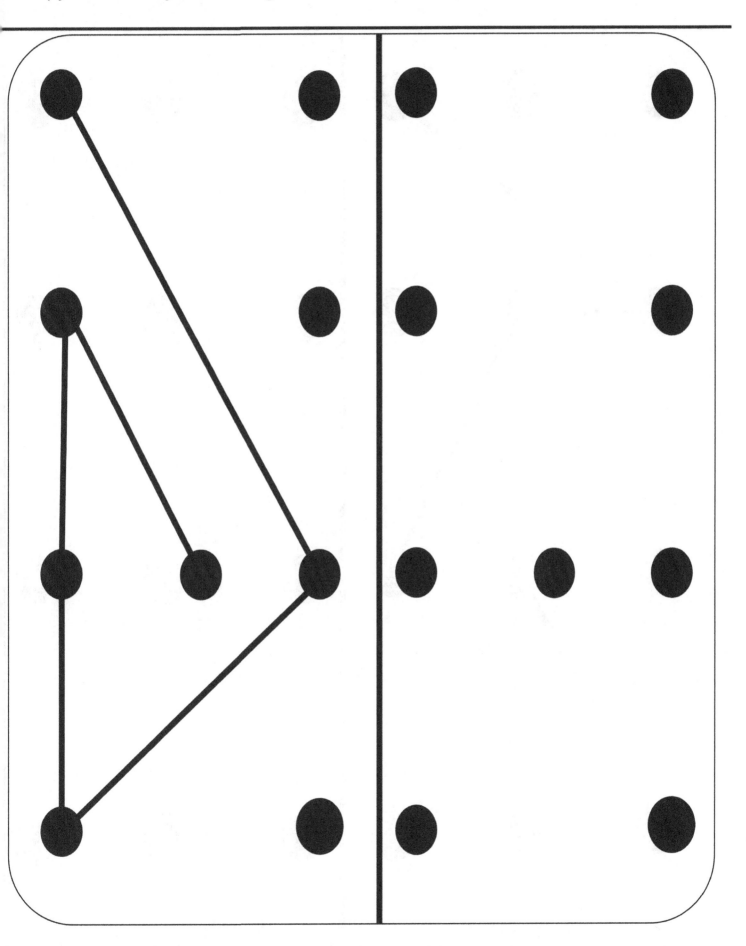

Copy the Trail

Copy the route by connecting the dots.

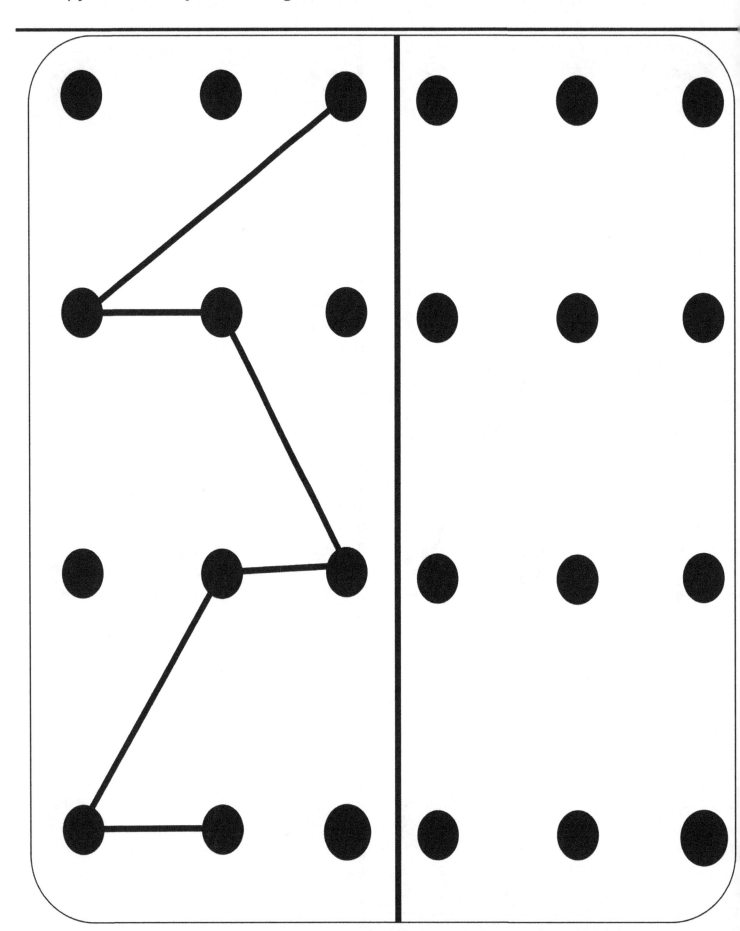

Odd One Out

How This Helps

This exercise is designed to help you improve your categorization, discrimination, and visual perceptual skills. By identifying the item that does not belong in a group, you'll need to analyze and compare the properties of different objects, focusing on the distinguishing features among a set of items. This process will help enhance your cognitive abilities, attention, problem-solving skills, and cognitive flexibility, as you'll need to shift your attention between multiple items to determine which one stands out. By strengthening these cognitive skills, you may experience improvements in your language and communication abilities, as well as in your everyday functioning.

Instructions

1) Look at the given set of items, which are usually presented in a group or list.

2) Observe each item carefully, noting their features or characteristics. Identify any commonalities or patterns among most of the items in the group.

3) Find the item that does not share the same features, characteristics, or patterns as the others. This item is the "odd one out."

4) Circle the odd one out.

5) Remember to take your time and pay attention to the details of each item. The key to successfully completing the exercise is to focus on the differences and determine which item doesn't fit the pattern or category shared by the other items in the group.

Odd One Out

Find the object that does not belong and circle it.

Odd One Out

Find the object that does not belong and circle it.

1.

2.

3.

4.

Odd One Out

Find the object that does not belong and circle it.

1.

2.

3.

Odd One Out

Find the object that does not belong and circle it.

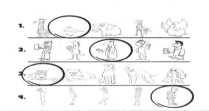

Odd One Out

Find the object that does not belong and circle it.

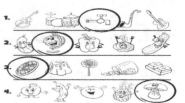

Odd One Out

Find the object that does not belong and circle it.

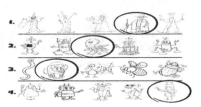

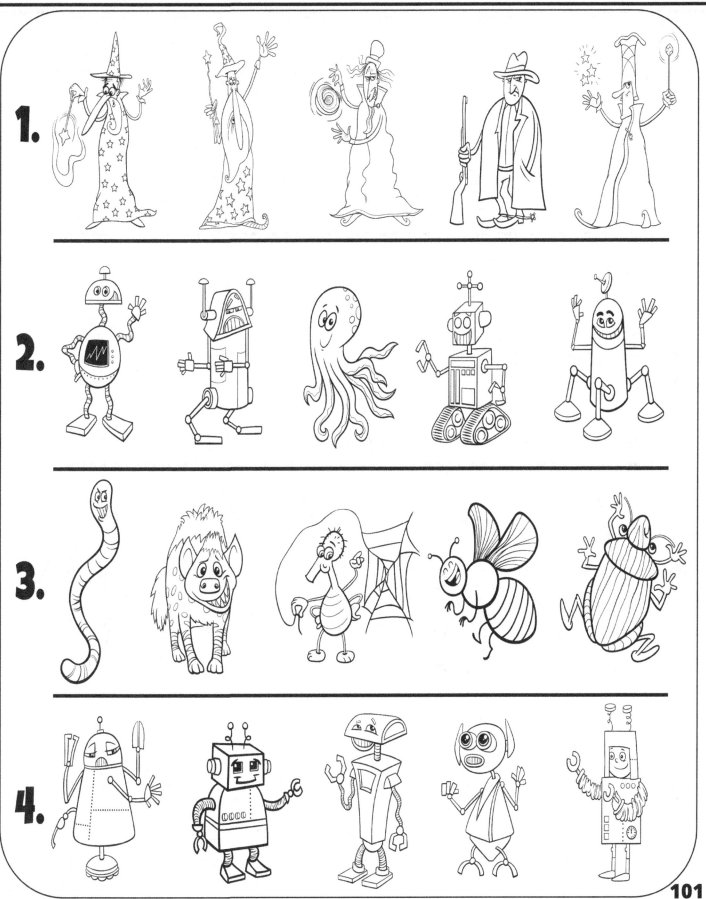

1.

2.

3.

4.

Odd One Out

Find the object that does not belong and circle it.

Odd One Out

Find the object that does not belong and circle it.

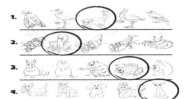

1.

2.

3.

4.

Odd One Out

Find the object that does not belong and circle it.

1.

2.

3.

4.

Odd One Out

Find the object that does not belong and circle it.

1.

2.

3.

4.

Hand Signals

How This Helps

In this new section on hand signals practice, you'll be asked to replicate various hand signals. This exercise can be beneficial for you because it helps improve your motor skills and hand-eye coordination. By focusing on replicating hand signals, you'll be working on your ability to understand and follow visual cues, which can strengthen the connections between your visual processing and motor functions.

Additionally, practicing hand signals may indirectly support your language recovery by enhancing your nonverbal communication skills. As you become more proficient in using and understanding hand signals, you may find it easier to express yourself and comprehend others, even when verbal communication is challenging. Overall, this exercise aims to boost your confidence and improve your communication abilities, both verbally and nonverbally.

Instructions

1) Look at the given hand signal,.
2) Carefully observe the position of the fingers, hand and wrist, as well as the overall shape and orientation of the hand signal.
3) Focus on the hand signal and try to create a mental image of it to help you remember its details.
4) Slowly raise your hand and attempt to replicate the hand signal by positioning your fingers, hand, and wrist in the same way as shown in the example.
5) Compare your hand signal with the example, and make any necessary adjustments to match it as closely as possible.
6) Practice the hand signal multiple times to reinforce the learning and improve your accuracy in replicating it.

Remember to be patient with yourself and take your time. Repetition and practice are essential for improving your motor skills and hand-eye coordination, as well as your ability to understand and use nonverbal communication effectively.

Improve motor skills and hand-eye coordination.

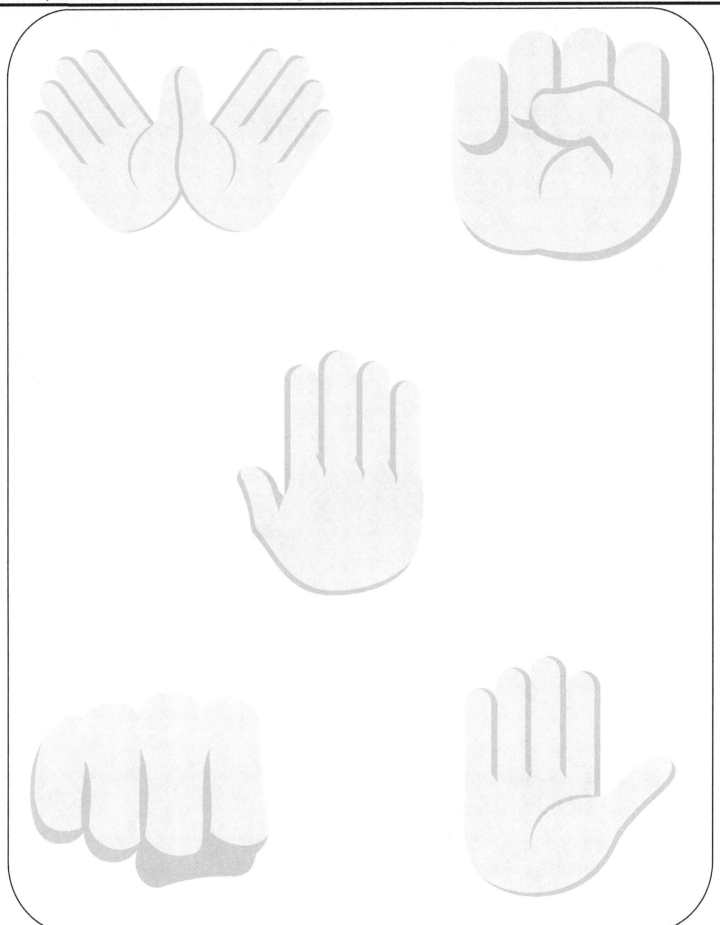

Improve motor skills and hand-eye coordination.

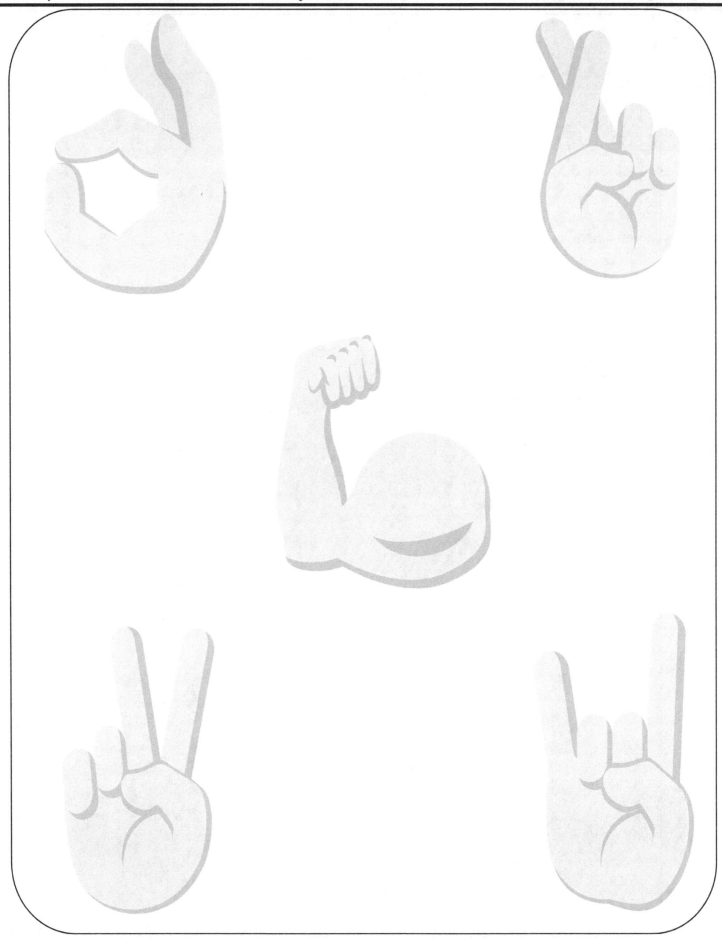

Improve motor skills and hand-eye coordination.

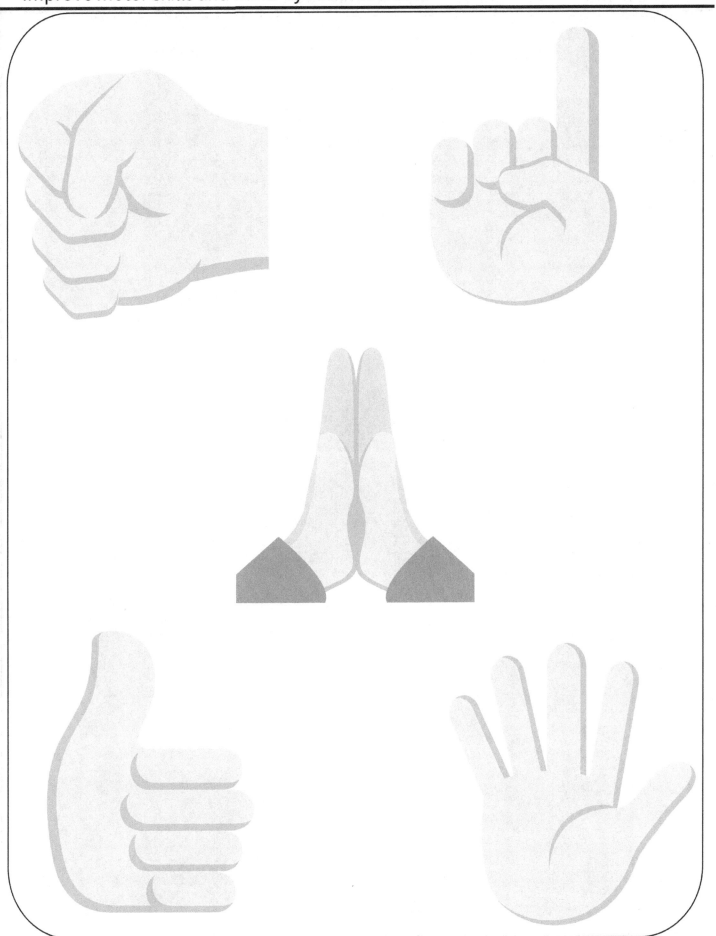

Improve motor skills and hand-eye coordination.

Improve motor skills and hand-eye coordination.

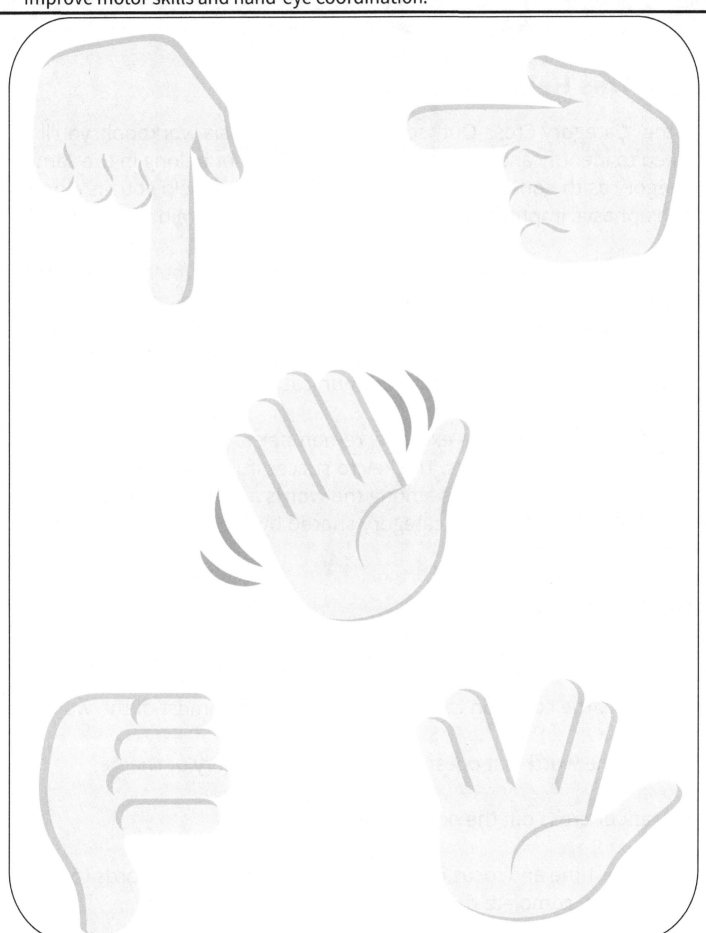

Category Cross-Out

How This Helps

In the "Category Cross-Out" section of your aphasia workbook, you'll be asked to identify and mark the word that does not belong in the same category as the others. This exercise is designed to help you, as a person with aphasia, improve your categorization and discrimination skills.

By identifying the word that doesn't fit in the group, you'll be required to analyze and compare the properties of different words, which in turn helps enhance your cognitive abilities, attention, and problem-solving skills. This improvement in cognitive functions may contribute to your language recovery and overall communication abilities.

As you work through this exercise, remember to take your time and concentrate on the details. The key to successfully completing the task is to focus on the differences among the words and determine which one does not fit the pattern or category shared by the other words in the group.

Instructions

1) Read the list of words presented in a group.

2) Identify the common category or theme among most of the words.

3) Spot the word that doesn't fit within the category or theme.

4) Mark or cross out the odd one out.

Take your time and focus on the differences among the words to successfully complete the exercise.

Category Cross-Out

Identify and mark the word that does not belong to the same category as the others

Apple	Carrot	Banana	Orange
Red	Blue	Square	Yellow
Dog	Elephant	Rose	Giraffe
Mars	Jupiter	Earth	Pencil
January	April	July	Table
Guitar	Trumpet	Violin	Shoe
Dolphin	Shark	Octopus	Tree
Toyota	Nissan	Chocolate	Honda
Oak	Pine	Maple	Tiger
Pants	Shirt	Hat	Sandwich
Toaster	Blender	Oven	Parrot
Broccoli	Cabbage	Potato	Chair
Square	Triangle	Circle	Rabbit
Football	Baseball	Tennis	Laptop
Sparrow	Eagle	Parrot	Watch
Rose	Tulip	Sunflower	Elephant
France	Brazil	Canada	Water
Coffee	Tea	Juice	Lamp
Math	Science	History	Zebra
Table	Chair	Sofa	Apple

Category Cross-Out

Identify and mark the word that does not belong to the same category as the others

Pear	Grape	Chicken	Strawberry
Green	Triangle	Purple	Brown
Horse	Cat	Banana	Lion
Venus	Saturn	Mercury	Car
February	August	Wednesday	March
Drum	Flute	Harp	Book
Whale	Seal	Starfish	Lobster
Ford	Chevrolet	Bicycle	Mercedes
Birch	Willow	Cedar	Bicycle
Jacket	Gloves	Scarf	Candle
Microwave	Fridge	Stove	Dolphin
Peas	Lettuce	Turnip	Radio
Rectangle	Hexagon	Oval	Dog
Basketball	Hockey	Golf	Telephone
Owl	Rooster	Penguin	Camera
Daisy	Lily	Dandelion	Giraffe
Italy	Spain	Shoe	Germany
Milk	Soda	Water	Desk
English	Geography	Art	Cheetah
Desk	Bed	Wardrobe	Pear

Category Cross-Out

Identify and mark the word that does not belong to the same category as the others

Melon	Raspberry	Bell	Blueberry
Gold	Octagon	Silver	Bronze
Zebra	Squirrel	Cup	Fox
Pluto	Neptune	Uranus	Fork
June	Sunday	October	December
Piano	Clarinet	Trumpet	Flower
Crab	Jellyfish	Seagull	Shrimp
BMW	Audi	Sandwich	Volkswagen
Palm	Fir	Redwood	Lightbulb
Tie	Socks	Belt	Pizza
Washer	Dryer	Oven	Elephant
Carrot	Celery	Onion	Chair
Pentagon	Circle	Diamond	Cow
Rugby	Badminton	Cricket	Clock
Swan	Goose	Ostrich	Lamp
Orchid	Marigold	Rose	Cat
Australia	Hat	China	India
Beer	Coffee	Wine	Pencil
Biology	Algebra	Chemistry	Horse
Couch	Armchair	Dresser	Orange

Identify and mark the word that does not belong to the same category as the others

Peach	Kiwi	Plum	Television
White	Cylinder	Black	Pink
Giraffe	Mouse	Hammer	Badger
Earth	Mars	Ring	Venus
April	July	Calculator	November
Violin	Trombone	Cello	Mountain
Shark	Tuna	Butterfly	Salmon
Tesla	Jaguar	Pillow	Ferrari
Cypress	Elm	Magnolia	Scissors
Hat	Watch	Necklace	Apple
Dishwasher	Refrigerator	Radio	Blender
Kale	Broccoli	Tomato	Notebook
Star	Crescent	Triangle	Penguin
Tennis	Volleyball	Bread	Soccer
Vulture	Hawk	Pigeon	Hairbrush
Hyacinth	Violet	Carnation	Mouse
Russia	Brazil	Coffee	Japan
Whiskey	Tea	Rum	Door
Physics	Calculus	Grammar	Strawberry
Lamp	Table	Nightstand	Grape

Identify and mark the word that does not belong to the same category as the others

Lemon	Lime	Cucumber	Tangerine
Yellow	Sphere	Orange	Red
Hedgehog	Ferret	Spoon	Otter
Jupiter	Mercury	Coat	Saturn
May	September	Calculator	February
Harp	Saxophone	Drums	River
Eel	Dolphin	Clam	Seaweed
Cadillac	Hyundai	Umbrella	Subaru
Beech	Ash	Maple	Pen
Ring	Earrings	Bracelet	Grapes
Freezer	Mixer	Toaster	Kangaroo
Spinach	Cauliflower	Asparagus	Stapler
Cube	Ellipse	Rectangle	Elephant
Swimming	Jogging	Climbing	Chair
Albatross	Dove	Sparrow	Toothbrush
Daffodil	Sunflower	Jasmine	Frog
USA	Mexico	Pasta	Canada
Gin	Juice	Vodka	Guitar
History	Literature	Geology	Pear
Mirror	Wardrobe	Bookshelf	Cherry

Identify and mark the word that does not belong to the same category as the others

Mango	Pineapple	Potato	Papaya
Blue	Pyramid	Green	Purple
Koala	Raccoon	Plate	Bobcat
Saturn	Uranus	Boot	Neptune
August	Monday	January	March
Trumpet	Flute	Oboe	Lake
Stingray	Seahorse	Snail	Coral
Lexus	Kia	Wallet	Nissan
Cedar	Oak	Birch	Balloon
Shoe	Glove	Hat	Banana
Heater	Vacuum	Microwave	Cheetah
Raddish	Eggplant	Beet	Keyboard
Hexagon	Octagon	Square	Giraffe
Diving	Jumping	Running	Lamp
Flamingo	Crow	Heron	Ruler
Lilac	Poppy	Orchid	Dolphin
Egypt	Peru	Guitar	Argentina
Sake	Milk	Champagne	Window
Anatomy	Geometry	Zoology	Melon
Cabinet	Drawer	Chair	Grapefruit

Category Cross-Out

Identify and mark the word that does not belong to the same category as the others

Grape	Apple	Orange	Desk
Pink	Circle	Gold	Blue
Seal	Beaver	Bottle	Bear
Mars	Earth	Hat	Venus
June	Friday	April	July
Clarinet	Violin	Cello	Pond
Salmon	Trout	Rose	Catfish
Ford	Audi	Shoe	BMW
Pine	Spruce	Elm	Clock
Boot	Sandal	Glove	Slipper
Oven	Sink	Grill	Tiger
Corn	Carrot	Lettuce	Radio
Triangle	Oval	Square	Lion
Jumping	Walking	Swimming	Table
Eagle	Robin	Finch	Brush
Tulip	Daisy	Rose	Monkey
France	Italy	Spoon	Spain
Rum	Wine	Ale	Lamp
Botany	Algebra	Biology	Peach
Shelf	Desk	Bed	Pear

Category Cross-Out

Identify and mark the word that does not belong to the same category as the others

Cherry	Chair	Plum	Peach
Silver	Rectangle	Copper	Gold
Rabbit	Tiger	Cup	Wolf
Mercury	Mars	Scarf	Pluto
September	Thursday	May	October
Banjo	Drum	Harp	Stream
Bass	Cod	Lily	Mackerel
Toyota	Mazda	Boot	Chevrolet
Birch	Pine	Fir	Bag
Shirt	Pants	Tie	Grape
Dishwasher	Stove	Toaster	Zebra
Peas	Spinach	Broccoli	Clock
Sphere	Pentagon	Circle	Fox
Running	Dancing	Skating	Apple
Hawk	Swallow	Finch	Bowl
Iris	Daisy	Petunia	Snake
Japan	China	Notebook	Korea
Tea	Coffee	Whiskey	Rock
Physics	Chemistry	English	Banana
Table	Cupboard	Dresser	Orange

Category Cross-Out

Identify and mark the word that does not belong to the same category as the others

Apricot	Kiwi	Apple	Pencil
Bronze	Square	Brass	Ruby
Panda	Lion	Glass	Fox
Moon	Sun	Tie	Earth
August	Sunday	July	February
Tuba	Piano	Cello	River
Herring	Tuna	Tulip	Sardine
Volvo	Tesla	Pen	Honda
Oak	Willow	Maple	Shoe
Dress	Skirt	Coat	Orange
Blender	Fridge	Stove	Dolphin
Lettuce	Tomato	Celery	Notebook
Star	Crescent	Oval	Cat
Cycling	Skiing	Rowing	Hat
Sparrow	Falcon	Canary	Cup
Lavender	Daisy	Bear	Rose
India	Brazil	Ball	Argentina
Cider	Juice	Coffee	Wall
French	Biology	Spanish	Peach
Mirror	Sofa	Bed	Apple

Identify and mark the word that does not belong to the same category as the others

Papaya	Lime	Lemon	Desk
Green	Ellipse	Turquoise	Red
Walrus	Otter	Flask	Seal
Neptune	Jupiter	Necklace	Saturn
March	Tuesday	June	January
Flute	Cymbal	Oboe	Lake
Cod	Flounder	Geranium	Haddock
Buick	Subaru	Brush	Hyundai
Redwood	Alder	Elm	Key
Sock	Glove	Scarf	Lemon
Microwave	Oven	Sink	Eagle
Kale	Cabbage	Cauliflower	Radio
Rhombus	Triangle	Circle	Zebra
Hiking	Reading	Fishing	Spoon
Heron	Duck	Goose	Bowl
Lilac	Azalea	Rose	Deer
USA	Germany	Hammer	Mexico
Lager	Wine	Ale	Door
History	Math	Geography	Grape
Nightstand	Dresser	Chair	Kiwi

Identify and mark the word that does not belong to the same category as the others

Grapefruit	Orange	Pear	Table
Cyan	Hexagon	Indigo	Violet
Sloth	Monkey	Bottle	Tiger
Mars	Venus	Glove	Uranus
April	Saturday	October	May
Horn	Trombone	Violin	Creek
Salmon	Mackerel	Daffodil	Trout
Dodge	Ford	Notebook	Nissan
Pine	Aspen	Birch	Ring
Shoe	Belt	Hat	Strawberry
Freezer	Oven	Toaster	Giraffe
Turnip	Potato	Beet	Lamp
Square	Pentagon	Octagon	Horse
Jumping	Writing	Dancing	Cup
Albatross	Sparrow	Hawk	Pen
Tulip	Iris	Poppy	Frog
Italy	England	Hammer	Spain
Gin	Coffee	Wine	Brick
Zoology	Physics	Chemistry	Potato
Desk	Sofa	Bench	Blueberry

Category Fill-In

How it Helps

Categorical fill-in exercises can be helpful to improve their ability to organize and categorize information. These exercises can also aid in the development of language skills, including vocabulary, word finding, and sentence construction. By categorizing items into specific groups, individuals with aphasia can practice cognitive skills such as attention, memory, and problem-solving, which can be impacted by brain injury or stroke.

In addition, categorization exercises can also help individuals with aphasia to improve their ability to use language functionally. By organizing words and concepts into categories, individuals with aphasia can more easily access and express their thoughts and ideas. This can help to improve communication with others and increase confidence in their ability to communicate effectively.

Overall, categorization exercises can be an effective way for individuals with aphasia to improve their language and cognitive skills, and ultimately, their ability to communicate effectively in everyday life.

Instructions

Look at the list of words at the top of the page. There are 30 words in total, with 5 words from each of the 6 categories

1) Using the words at the top of the page, write each word in the correct category by placing it under the corresponding category.

2) Check your answers to make sure each word is in the correct category.

3) If you have any difficulty categorizing a word, try to think of what category it might fit in based on its characteristics or context.

Category Fill-In

Place the words in their appropriate category.

Tequila	Chardonnay	Leather	Wool	Catfish	Riesling
Cod	Muskie	Velvet	Scotch	Tweed	Fedora
Fleece	Suede	Trout	Bass	Gin	Mahi-mahi
Cabernet	Sauvignon	Merlot	Nylon	Halibut	Linen
Pumps	Flounder	Loafers	Pinot	Silk	Sneakers

TYPES OF FABRIC

_____

_____

_____

TYPES OF HATS

_____

_____

_____

TYPES OF FISH

_____

_____

_____

TYPES OF ALCOHOL

_____

_____

_____

TYPES OF WINE

_____

_____

_____

TYPES OF FOOTWEAR

_____

_____

_____

Category Fill-In

Place the words in their appropriate category.

Lollipop   Fettuccine   Candy Corn   Jellyfish   Salami   Twix
Scrabble   Brie   Dolphin   Snickers   Opal   Monopoly
Gorgonzola   Tootsie Roll Blue Cheese   Linguine   Skittles   Parmesan
Basalt   Crayon   Bocce   Chess   Clam   Shale
Seaweed   Marble   Sandstone   Granite   Candy Cane   Kraken

BOARD GAMES

_____

_____

_____

_____

SEA CREATURES

_____

_____

_____

_____

TYPES OF ROCKS

_____

_____

_____

TYPES OF CANDY

_____

_____

_____

TYPES OF PASTA

_____

_____

_____

TYPES OF CHEESE

_____

_____

_____

Category Fill-In

Place the words in their appropriate category.

Enzyme　　Cabin　　Guitar　　Turkey　　Truck　　Scooter
Emerald　　Amber　　Kiwi　　Ravioli　　Zucchini　　Nurse
Noodle　　Salmon　　Diamond　　Sapphire　　Pearl　　Chicken
Avocado　　Carrot　　Lemon　　Venus　　Stomach　　Uranus
Cherry　　Jupiter　　Lawyer　　Train　　Painter　　Chef

VEHICLES

_____

_____

_____

_____

PROFESSIONS

_____

_____

_____

_____

PLANETS

_____

_____

_____

BODY ORGANS

_____

_____

_____

GEMSTONES

_____

_____

_____

TYPES OF CUISINE

_____

_____

_____

Category Fill-In

Place the words in their appropriate category.

Red   Circle   Ant   Christmas   Hurricane   Happy
Blue Square   Butterfly   Halloween   Tornado   Sad
Green Triangle Ladybug   Thanksgiving   Earthquake   Angry
Yellow Rectangle Grasshopper Easter   Flood   Excited
Purple Hexagon Bee   Valentine's Day Wildfire   Nervous

COLORS

_____

_____

_____

_____

SHAPES

_____

_____

_____

_____

INSECTS

_____

_____

_____

HOLIDAYS

_____

_____

_____

NATURAL DISASTERS

_____

_____

_____

EMOTIONS

_____

_____

_____

Category Fill-In

Place the words in their appropriate category.

Oak	Carnation	Sushi	Birch	Pine	Redwood
Hamburger	Flute	Bracelet	Ring	Brooch	Watch
Butterfly	Necklace	Willow	Climbing	Fencing	Pasta
Earrings	Snowboarding	Archery	Tacos	Rafting	Pizza
Yacht	Tugboat	Submarine	Sailboat	Cruise Ship	Canoe

TREES

_____

_____

_____

_____

JEWELRY

_____

_____

_____

_____

FOOD

_____

_____

_____

LAND ACTIVITIES

_____

_____

_____

BOATS

_____

_____

_____

FLOWERS

_____

_____

_____

Category Fill-In

Place the words in their appropriate category.

Lettuce	Eye	Carrot	Arm	Juice
Shoes	Sunny	Soccer	Basketball	Windy
Tea	Swimming	Hat	Cloudy	Water
Tennis	Coffee	Snow	Socks	Milk
Nose	Tomato	Leg	Broccoli	Pants

VEGETABLES

_____

_____

_____

_____

SPORTS

_____

_____

_____

_____

BEVERAGES

_____

_____

_____

BODY PARTS

_____

_____

_____

WEATHER

_____

_____

_____

CLOTHING

_____

_____

_____

Place the words in their appropriate category.

Halloween   Cowboys   49ers   Wide-Leg   Packers   Seahawks

August   Dachshund   Bulldog   Gibbous   Siberian Husky   New Year's Eve

Buddhism   January   April   North America   November   Christianity

Golden Retriever   Judaism   Hinduism   Camaro   Islam   December

Margarita   Cosmopolitan   Old Fashioned   Atlantic   Mojito   October

---

HOLIDAYS

_____

_____

_____

_____

PLANES

_____

_____

_____

_____

PANT STYLES

_____

_____

_____

PHASES OF THE MOON

_____

_____

_____

OCEANS

_____

_____

_____

CONTINENTS

_____

_____

_____

Category Fill-In

Place the words in their appropriate category.

Venus   Maine Coon   Brown Recluse   Cardinal   Jumping Spider   Washington

Black Widow   Clinton   Humerus   Mars   Hawk   Neptune

Obama   Wolf Spider   Daddy Long Legs   Tibia   Roosevelt   American Robin

Shynx   Fibula   Jefferson   Siamese   Bengal   Saturn

Bald Eagle   Persian   Blue Jay   Jupiter   Skull   Femur

PRESIDENTS

_____

_____

_____

_____

PLANETS

_____

_____

_____

_____

SPIDERS

_____

_____

_____

BIRDS

_____

_____

_____

CATS

_____

_____

_____

BONES

_____

_____

_____

Category Fill-In

Place the words in their appropriate category.

Impala	Airbus	Piper	Wide-Leg	Skinny	Boeing
Arctic	Pacific	Antarctica	Gibbous	Crescent	Africa
Cessna	Waxing	Full	North America	Corvette	Straight
Asia	Mustang	Southern	Camaro	Indian	Embraer
Bootcut	Flare	Europe	Atlantic	Waning	Challenged

CARS

_____

_____

_____

_____

PLANES

_____

_____

_____

PANT STYLES

_____

_____

_____

PHASES OF THE MOON

_____

_____

_____

OCEANS

_____

_____

_____

CONTINENTS

_____

_____

_____

Basic Functions

Name the word that has each function.

What do you do with a spoon?_____

What do you do with a pencil?_____

What do you do with a toothbrush?_____

What do you do with a bed? _____

What do you do with a coat? _____

What do you do with a cup? _____

What do you do with a fork? _____

What do you do with a hat? _____

What do you do with a shoe? _____

What do you do with a ruler? _____

What do you do with a calculator? _____

What do you do with a map?_____

What do you do with a microscope? _____

What do you do with a thermometer?_____

What do you do with a timer?_____

Comprehension

Math and number comprehension.

What is the next number after 5? _____

What number comes before 4? _____

What number comes after 9? _____

Which number is greater: 7 or 5?_____

What number comes between 2 and 4?_____

Which number is smaller: 8 or 10? _____

What number is twice as much as 5?_____

What number is three times as much as 2?_____

What is the difference between 2 and 5? _____

What number comes between 6 and 8?_____

How many digits are there in the number 123?_____

What number comes before 5? _____

Which number is bigger: 6 or 3?_____

If you add 2 and 3, what is the total?_____

How many sides does a square have?_____

Convergent Naming

Provide the name of the object or concept that matches the description.

Green, used for cutting grass, makes a buzzing sound _____

Round, has numbers, used to tell time_____

Made of glass, used for drinking water, can be filled with ice _____

Has wings, flies, eats nectar _____

Used for cleaning teeth, often made of plastic, has bristles_____

Small, used for writing, contains ink, can be disposable _____

Tiny grains, found on beach, often hot under the sun _____

Used for playin music, has strings, comes in many shapes and sizes _____

Tall, has bark, proovides shade _____

Fluffy, purrs, chases mice, has nine lives_____

Clear, falls from clouds, plants need it _____

Cold, creamy, comes in flavors like chocolate and vanilla _____

Four wheels, carries passengers, driven on roads_____

Red or green, fruit, keeps the doctor away _____

Loud, follows lightning, sound from the sky_____

Furry, barks, man's best friend_____

Bright, warms the earth, rises in the morning_____

Convergent Naming

Provide the name of the object or concept that matches the description.

Worn around the wrist, can be shiny, tells time_____

Bright at night, made of wax, has a wick_____

Shiny, falls from the sky at night, make a wish on one_____

Warm, brewed, can be black or with cream _____

Large, has giant ears, has a trunk and tusks _____

Flick it to start, gives light, must be careful with it _____

Fluffy, white, used on beds for comfort_____

Rings when there's a visitor, triggered by a button_____

Worn on the face, helps to see better_____

Delivers mail, wears a uniform, drives or walks_____

Soft, cuddly, a child's bedtime companion _____

Large body of water, smaller than an ocean _____

Driven on tracks, has many carriages, has a conductor _____

A flower, often red, a symbol of love, has thorns_____

Frothy, served in pints, often golden_____

Worn on the head, blocks sun from eyes_____

Stringed instrument, has a bow, elegant sound_____

Divergent Naming: Categories

Name items in each category

KITCHEN APPLIANCES

_____

_____

_____

_____

EMOTIONS

_____

_____

_____

INSECTS

_____

_____

_____

SEAFOOD

_____

_____

_____

_____

BANDS

_____

_____

_____

_____

MODES OF TRANSPORTATION

_____

_____

_____

LANDMARKS

_____

_____

_____

TYPES OF PASTA

_____

_____

_____

_____

Divergent Naming: Categories

Name items in each category

MUSICAL INSTRUMENTS

_____

_____

_____

_____

COLORS

_____

_____

_____

_____

FRUIT

_____

_____

_____

_____

GEMSTONES

_____

_____

_____

VEGETABLES

_____

_____

_____

_____

ANIMALS

_____

_____

_____

_____

FURNITURE

_____

_____

_____

_____

DRINKS

_____

_____

_____

Synonyms

Choose a different word that has the same or similar meaning as the given word.
Use the new word to create a sentence that makes sense.
This will help you practice using different words and improve your vocabulary

1. Happy _____

2. Fun _____

3. Big _____

4. Small _____

5. Fast _____

6. Slow _____

7. Cold _____

8. Hot _____

9. Good _____

10. Bad _____

11. Pretty _____

12. Ugly _____

13. Tasty _____

14. Boring _____

16. Loud _____

17. Quiet _____

19. Hard _____

20. Soft _____

Antonyms

An antonym is a word that has the opposite meaning of another word. For example, "hot" and "cold" are antonyms, as are "big" and "small." Use an antonym from the words below to make a sentence.

1. Heavy _____

2. Hot _____

3. Up _____

4. Right _____

5. Fast _____

6. Bright _____

7. Near _____

8. Full _____

9. Easy _____

10. Wet _____

11. Young _____

12. Dark _____

13. Clean _____

14. Open _____

16. Big _____

17. Thick _____

19. Strong _____

20. Start _____

Homonyms

Homonyms are words that are spelled and pronounced the same way but have different meanings. An example of a homonym is the word "bat," which can refer to a flying mammal or a piece of sports equipment used to hit a ball. Both meanings are spelled and pronounced the same way, but have different definitions.

INSTRUCTIONS: Fill in the blanks with the correct homonym.

She wore a _____ dress to the party. (blue/blew)

The _____ is a type of fish. (bass/base)

The _____ of the church was beautiful. (isle/aisle)

He _____ a new book yesterday. (read/red)

I need to _____ the lawn this weekend. (mow/moe)

The _____ was ringing loudly. (bell/belle)

We will _____ the bread in the oven for 30 minutes. (bake/brake)

The _____ was very good at math. (sum/son)

The _____ is a measurement of weight. (ounce/once)

The _____ was growing in the garden. (bean/been)

The _____ of the mountain was covered in snow. (peak/peek)

He _____ the ball to the outfield. (threw/through)

The _____ was used to cut the cake. (knife/nice)

The _____ was a popular movie star. (idol/idle)

He _____ his keys on the kitchen counter. (settled/meddled)

The _____ of the train tracks was dangerous. (knot/not)

She _____ her hair with a brush. (combs/comes)

The _____ was reading a book on the bench. (reader/reeder)

The _____ was used to make a fire. (match/match)

The _____ was painted a bright shade of yellow. (board/bored)

Homonyms

Homonyms are words that are spelled and pronounced the same way but have different meanings. An example of a homonym is the word "bat," which can refer to a flying mammal or a piece of sports equipment used to hit a ball. Both meanings are spelled and pronounced the same way, but have different definitions.

INSTRUCTIONS: Fill in the blanks with the correct homonym.

She had a _____ personality. (bold/bowled)

He _____ the mountain without any equipment. (climbed/crime)

The _____ was suspended from school. (principal/principle)

She had a _____ day at work. (bear/bare)

He _____ a lot of weight in a short amount of time. (lost/lust)

The _____ of the play was very dramatic. (scene/seen)

The _____ of the house was covered in ivy. (wall/waul)

The _____ of the car was dented in the accident. (fender/vendor)

She has a _____ complexion. (fair/fare)

The _____ was filled with a delicious soup. (bowl/boll)

The _____ was very difficult to solve. (puzzle/puddle)

The _____ was covered in mud. (boot/bute)

The _____ of the play was very emotional. (tear/tear)

The _____ was filled with diamonds. (mine/min)

The _____ of the church was decorated for Christmas. (alter/altar)

He had a _____ look on his face. (grim/grin)

The _____ was very old and had a lot of history. (ruin/ruen)

The _____ was made of silver. (ware/wear)

The _____ was very intelligent. (genius/genes)

The _____ of the necklace was broken. (clasp/claps)

Compound Words

Compound words are made up of two or more words that are joined together to create a new word with a new meaning.
For example, "air" and "port" can be combined to form "airport," which refers to a place where airplanes take off and land..

Draw a line to match the first part of the compound word with the second part.

water	walk
black	time
hair	stop
snow	shine
air	shelf
door	shake
sun	ring
mail	port
night	board
cross	paste
tooth	man
ice	flower
ear	man
tooth	fall
fire	cream
sun	coat
book	brush
bus	port
rain	box
hand	bell

Cross | walk
Night | time
Bus | stop
Sun | shine
Book | shelf
Hand | shake
Ear | ring
Air | port
Black | board
Tooth | paste
Fire | man
Snow | man
Sun | flower
Water | fall
Ice | cream
Rain | coat
Tooth | brush
Hair | brush
Mail | box
Door | bell

Compound Words

Compound words are made up of two or more words that are joined together to create a new word with a new meaning.
For example, "air" and "port" can be combined to form "airport," which refers to a place where airplanes take off and land..

Draw a line to match the first part of the compound word with the second part.

house	chair
snow	fish
fire	plane
cup	ball
wheel	skate
ear	berry
arm	chair
blue	glasses
ice	mare
fire	truck
hair	house
sea	drum
jelly	light
moon	works
snow	cut
dog	mark
night	boat
sun	flake
air	chair
book	shell

Wheel | chair
Jelly | fish
Air | plane
Snow | ball
Cup | cake
Blue | berry
Ice | skate
Sun | glasses
Night | mare
Fire | truck
Dog | house
Ear | drum
Moon | light
Fire | works
Hair | cut
Book | mark
House | boat
Snow | flake
Arm | chair
Sea | shell

Rhyming Words

Rhyming words are words that have the same or similar sound at the end of their last syllable. When two or more words have a similar ending sound, they are said to rhyme. For example, "cat" and "hat" are rhyming words, as are "dog" and "frog," "tree" and "bee," and so on.

Draw a line to match the rhyming word on the left to the right.

bird	hat
tree	frog
book	bee
light	spoon
boot	hen
rain	fox
mouse	wig
pig	bear
cake	word
dog	truck
pen	star
fish	kite
cat	tall
bell	train
duck	cook
box	hat
chair	house
car	snake
ball	dish
moon	suit

Cat hat
Dog frog
Tree bee
Moon spoon
Pen hen
Box fox
Pig wig
Chair bear
Bird word
Duck truck
Car star
Light kite
Bell shell
Rain train
Book cook
Ball tall
Mouse house
Cake snake
Fish dish
Boot suit

Rhyming Words

Rhyming words are words that have the same or similar sound at the end of their last syllable. When two or more words have a similar ending sound, they are said to rhyme. For example, "cat" and "hat" are rhyming words, as are "dog" and "frog," "tree" and "bee," and so on.

Draw a line to match the rhyming word on the left to the right.

fear	bed
pen	wrist
tongue	ten
plan	pack
frown	can
coat	class
clock	dear
mask	chair
sheep	save
snack	mail
night	boat
red	right
sale	clown
wave	task
truck	luck
bait	sleep
mist	beach
hair	wait
glass	young
reach	rock

Glass - class
Night - right
Plan - can
Bait - wait
Clock - rock
Coat - boat
Fear - dear
Frown - clown
Hair - chair
Mask - task
Mist - wrist
Pen - ten
Reach - beach
Red - bed
Sale - mail
Sheep - sleep
Snack - pack
Tongue - young
Truck - luck
Wave - save

Collective Nouns

A collective noun is a word that refers to a group of individuals or things. For example, a "school" of fish, a "herd" of cows, a "swarm" of bees, and a "flock" of birds are all examples of collective nouns. They are used to describe a group of people, animals, or objects as a single entity. Improve your vocabulary and word recognition skills.

Draw a line to match the collective nouns.

Swarm of	Penguins
Gaggle of	Lions
Troop of	Musicians
Pod of	Sheep
Colony of	Snakes
Herd of	Cards
Army of	Bees
Pod of	Cows
Parliament of	Dolphins
Flock of	Ants
Pack of	Owls
Flock of	Monkeys
Colony of	Ships
Pride of	Fish
Pack of	Geese
Nest of	Elephants
Band of	Ants
Heard of	Whales
School of	wolves
Fleet of	Birds

School of | Fish
Herd of | Cows
Swarm of | Bees
Flock of | Birds
Colony of | Ants
Pod of | Dolphins
Pack of | Wolves
Pride of | Lions
Troop of | Monkeys
Gaggle of | Geese
Parliament of | Owls
Army of | Ants
Colony of | Penguins
Flock of | Sheep
Pod of | Whales
Nest of | Snakes
Pack of | Cards
Fleet of | Ships
Band of | Musicians
Herd of | Elephants

Collective Nouns

A collective noun is a word that refers to a group of individuals or things. For example, a "school" of fish, a "herd" of cows, a "swarm" of bees, and a "flock" of birds are all examples of collective nouns. They are used to describe a group of people, animals, or objects as a single entity. Improve your vocabulary and word recognition skills.

Draw a line to match the collective nouns.

Bunch of	Vultures
Pack of	Whales
Pride of	Insects
Army of	Lions
Bevy of	Geese
Colony of	Grapes
Pod of	Peacocks
Troop of	Beauties
Flock of	Puppies
Gaggle of	Swans
Parliament of	Activity
Band of	Thieves
Cloud of	Gulls
Litter of	Dancers
Hive of	Peacocks
Den of	Dogs
Muster of	Giraffes
School of	Rooks
Tower of	Soldiers
Committee of	Peas

Bunch of | Grapes
Pack of | Dogs
Pride of | Peacocks
Army of | Soldiers
Bevy of | Beauties
Colony of | Gulls
Pod of | Peas
Troop of | Dancers
Flock of | Geese
Gaggle of | Swans
Parliament of | Rooks
Band of | Thieves
Cloud of | Insects
Litter of | Puppies
Hive of | Activity
Den of | Lions
Muster of | Peacocks
School of | Whales
Tower of | Giraffes
Committee of | Vultures

Phrase Completion

Complete the phrase with a possible word or phrase that makes sense.
There may be more than one correct answer for each phrase.
Be creative and use your own words if you can't think of an obvious answer.

Use your own words and creativity to complete each phrase.

The early bird catches the _____

A penny for your _____

When in Rome, do as the _____

It's raining cats and _____

Don't judge a book by its _____

An apple a day keeps the _____

A watched pot never _____

You can't teach an old _____

When the going gets tough, the tough get _____

A rolling stone gathers no _____

All's fair in love and _____

You can lead a horse to water, but you can't make it _____

Two heads are better than _____

Actions speak louder than _____

Every cloud has a silver _____

Where there's smoke, there's _____

The grass is always greener on the other _____

Don't count your chickens before they're _____

Rome wasn't built in a _____

When life gives you lemons, make _____

Sentence Completion

Complete the sentence with the correct word that makes sense.
Choose the word from the options provided.
If you can't think of an obvious answer, use your best guess.

Be sure to read the sentence carefully before choosing the correct word.

I need to buy some _____.	milk	mail	mall
I can't find my _____.	hat	hot	hit
The sky is _____.	blue	flu	glue
The cat chased the _____.	mouse	house	blouse
I love to eat _____.	cake	make	take
The dog barks at the _____.	mailman	salesman	fisherman
She plays the _____.	piano	table	window
I wear a _____ on my head.	hat	bat	mat
I like to watch _____.	TV	DVD	VCR
He drove his _____ to work.	car	far	jar
The baby is crying in the _____.	crib	rib	bib
The bird is singing in the _____.	tree	knee	bee
I need to buy a new _____.	shirt	short	sport
She put on her _____.	shoes	blues	clues
I need to use the _____.	bathroom	bedroom	classroom
The sun is shining _____.	brightly	knightly	lightly
I have a _____ in my pocket.	coin	loin	join
The train is arriving at the _____.	station	nation	ration
He put the book on the _____.	table	cable	fable
She made a _____ for dinner.	cake	bake	take

Morphology

Complete the sentence with the correct word that makes sense.
Choose the word from the options provided.
If you can't think of an obvious answer, use your best guess.

Complete the sentences with the best word.

She was _____ about the weather.   unhappy|prehappy|antihappy

The baby was _____ when her mother left.   uncry|pre-cry|anticry

The team was _____ after winning.   overjoyed|underjoyed|misjoyed

The concert was _____ because of rain.   post-cancel|overcancel|uncanceled

The doctor prescribed an _____ medication. anti-inflammatory|pre-inflammatory|un-inflammatory

The movie was _____ because of violence.   unwatchable|overwatchable|post-watchable

The food tasted _____ because of salt. oversalted|undersalted|unsalted

The customer was _____ with the service.   dissatisfied|oversatisfied|unsatisfied

The flowers were _____ in sunlight. overbloomed|underbloomed|post-bloomed

The cat was _____ after eating.   overfull|underfull|post-full

The student was _____ about the test.   preanxious|overanxious|underanxious

The coffee was _____ because of sugar. oversweetened|postsweetened|unsweetened

The athlete was _____ after winning.   overactive|hyperactive|hypoactive

The painting was _____ because of colors. unattractive|overattractive|post-attractive

The dog was _____ because of noises.   oversensitive|insensitive|post-sensitive

The road was _____ because of traffic. overcongested|undercongested|uncongested

The child was _____ after getting a toy. hyperactive|hypoactive|overactive

The music was _____ because of melody. unrelaxing|overrelaxing|post-relaxing

The dish was _____ because of sauce. overspiced|underspiced|unspiced

The sky was _____ because of storm.   overcloudy|precloudy|undercloudy

"What" Questions

Answer "what" questions to boost your language and understanding. Think about each answer and either write it or say it aloud based on your comfort.

What is your favorite song?

What do you like to do on the weekends?

What animal is known as the king of the jungle?

What do you call the first meal of the day?

What holiday is celebrated on December 25th?

What planet is known as the "Red Planet"?

What do you wish to achieve by the end of this year?

What is the main ingredient in guacamole?

What color are strawberries?

What instrument has 88 keys and is played by Beethoven?

What sport uses a round, black and white ball?

What is your best childhood memory?

What is the name of the ship that famously sank in 1912 after hitting an iceberg?

What do you typically eat with cereal?

What is the color of a school bus?

What flowers are commonly associated with Valentine's Day?

What place is often referred to as "The Land Down Under"?

"Where" Questions

Answer "where" questions to boost your language and understanding. Think about each answer and either write it or say it aloud based on your comfort.

Where is the Eiffel Tower located?

Where do penguins primarily live?

Where is the heart located in the human body?

Where do we get honey from?

Where do kangaroos predominantly reside?

Where was the Declaration of Independence signed?

Where do you go to mail a package?

Where does the sun rise?

Where do you store frozen food at home?

Where do you go to borrow books?

Where can you deposit money into your bank account?

Where do bats hang during the day?

Where is Hollywood?

Where does Santa Claus live?

Where can you find the Pyramids?

Where do birds migrate to in the winter?

Where is Stonehenge located?

"Who" Questions

Answer "who" questions to boost your language and understanding. Think about each answer and either write it or say it aloud based on your comfort.

Who wrote "Romeo and Juliet"?

Who was the first president of the United States?

Who painted the Mona Lisa?

Who discovered gravity?

Who gave the "I Have a Dream" speech?

Who was the first person to walk on the moon?

Who is the mascot of Disney?

Who delivers mail to your house?

Who wears a big red suit and delivers presents at Christmas?

Who helps sick people and might give you medicine?

Who is the president on the $1 bill?

Who is the web-slinging superhero in New York City?

Who climbs up beanstalks in a fairy tale?

Who has a red nose and helps guide Santa's sleigh?

Who cuts and styles your hair at a salon?

Who helps you when you have a toothache?

Who bakes bread and pastries in a bakery?

Answer "when" questions to boost your language and understanding. Think about each answer and either write it or say it aloud based on your comfort.

When do we celebrate Halloween?

When do you have breakfast, in the morning or evening?

When is Valentine's Day?

When do birds typically migrate?

When is the first day of the year?

When do leaves fall from deciduous trees?

When is Independence Day in the USA?

When do we eat turkey and give thanks in the U.S.?

When does a baby take its first steps, at 1 week or around 1 year?

When do we give gifts and decorate a tree in December?

When do kids hunt for eggs, often made of chocolate?

When does the moon shine, day or night?

When do you celebrate your birthday?

When does the school day typically start?

When do we wear costumes and ask for candy?

When is New Year's Eve?

When do most people take a lunch break?

"How" Questions

Answer "how" questions to boost your language and understanding. Think about each answer and either write it or say it aloud based on your comfort.

How do you tie your shoes?

How do birds fly?

How do you boil water?

How do you brush your teeth?

How do you bake cookies?

How do you make lemonade?

How does a light turn on?

How do you open a door?

How do you ride a bicycle?

How do you write with a pen?

How do you clap your hands?

How do you plant a tree?

How do you put on a jacket?

How do you spread butter on bread?

How do you blow up a balloon?

How do you peel a banana?

How do you make a sandwich?

"Why" Questions

Answer "why" questions to boost your language and understanding. Think about each answer and either write it or say it aloud based on your comfort.

Why do we eat food?

Why does the moon shine at night?

Why do we wear shoes?

Why do plants need water?

Why do we brush our teeth?

Why do we sleep at night?

Why do we use umbrellas when it rains?

Why does an apple fall from a tree?

Why do people wear glasses?

Why do we say "bless you" when someone sneezes?

Why does ice melt in the sun?

Why do we go to school?

Why do we yawn?

Why do some birds migrate?

Why does chocolate melt in the sun?

Why do we wear seatbelts in cars?

Why do we put ice on a bruise?

Idiomatic Sentences

Practice explaining the meaning of idiomatic sentences to help improve your language skills and comprehension. Idioms are expressions with figurative meanings that are different from their literal meanings. For each idiom, take your time to think about its meaning and try to explain it in your own words.

The early bird catches the worm.

Don't put all your eggs in one basket.

It's raining cats and dogs outside.

She has a chip on her shoulder.

He's feeling under the weather today.

That costs an arm and a leg.

They're just adding fuel to the fire.

It takes two to tango.

He's barking up the wrong tree.

She let the cat out of the bag.

They're walking on eggshells around her.

It's a piece of cake.

He's been burning the candle at both ends.

She's in hot water now.

You can't judge a book by its cover.

He's been on cloud nine since he got the promotion.

She's the apple of her father's eye.

Don't count your chickens before they hatch.

Time flies when you're having fun.

He's the black sheep of the family.

Analogies

Practice completing analogies to help improve your language and comprehension skills. An analogy is a comparison between two things that are similar in some way. For each analogy, you will be provided with a pair of words that have a relationship, followed by a third word. Your task is to find the word that shares a similar relationship with the third word.

HOT is to COLD as BIG is to _____

BIRD is to FLY as FISH is to _____

DAY is to NIGHT as SUN is to _____

PEN is to WRITE as SCISSORS are to _____

SALT is to PEPPER as FORK is to _____

DOG is to BARK as CAT is to _____

SHIRT is to LAUNDRY as DISH is to _____

SUMMER is to WINTER as WARM is to _____

FOOT is to SHOE as HAND is to _____

RIVER is to BOAT as ROAD is to _____

EYES are to SEE as EARS are to _____

APPLES are to FRUIT as CARROTS are to _____

RAIN is to UMBRELLA as SUN is to _____

KING is to QUEEN as HUSBAND is to _____

MOUSE is to CHEESE as BEE is to _____

CAR is to GASOLINE as BICYCLE is to _____

FLOWER is to GARDEN as TREE is to _____

TEACHER is to SCHOOL as DOCTOR is to _____

SLEEP is to BED as COOK is to _____

BUTTERFLY is to CATERPILLAR as FROG is to _____

"Yes/No" Questions

Complete all the "yes/no" questions at your own pace. Remember, this exercise is designed to help you practice and improve your language and comprehension skills. The more you practice, the better you'll become at understanding and answering "yes/no" questions. These questions are designed to be answerd with either "yes" or "no."

Is water essential for human survival?

Are there twelve months in a year?

Can birds swim underwater?

Do plants produce oxygen?

Is the sky green?

Can elephants fly?

Does a week have 5 days?

Is snow hot?

Are there 60 minutes in an hour?

Can a car run without fuel?

Do humans have 10 fingers?

Is ice cream a type of vegetable?

Can a bicycle be ridden on water?

Is fire cold to the touch?

Are dogs considered to be domestic animals?

Can you read a book in complete darkness?

Do fish breathe air like humans?

Is pizza a traditional Italian dish?

Does a triangle have four sides?

Can airplanes travel underwater?

History Questions

Practice answering questions related to various locations around the world. These questions will help improve your language and comprehension skills, as well as your knowledge of geography. This exercise is designed to help you practice and improve your language and comprehension skills.

Who invented the light bulb?

Who was the first president of the United States?

Who discovered America in 1492?

In which year did World War I begin?

Who was the first man to walk on the moon?

What country did Christopher Columbus sail for?

Which civil rights activist refused to give up her seat on a bus in Montgomery, Alabama, in 1955?

Who is known for writing the Declaration of Independence?

What historical event took place in France in 1789?

Who was the first woman to fly solo across the Atlantic Ocean?

Which ship famously sank on its maiden voyage in 1912?

Who was the leader of the civil rights movement in the United States?

What wall divided Berlin from 1961 to 1989?

What was the name of the Russian space satellite that was the first to be launched into space?

Who is known as the "Father of the Constitution"?

Who was the famous physicist who developed the theory of relativity?

What was the name of the ancient Egyptian writing system?

What was the name of the famous Chinese dynasty known for its art and culture?

Which famous explorer is credited with circumnavigating the globe?

Who was the first emperor of the Roman Empire?

Spatial Awareness

Read the instructions for each box carefully to determine what you should draw or write in that box.
Pay attention to the orientation and location of each box to make sure you draw or write in the correct one.
Take your time and focus on accuracy rather than speed.

In the upper right box, write the letter "E".
In the lower left box, draw a circle.
In the upper left box, write the number "1".
In the lower right box, draw a triangle.

In the upper left box, draw a square.
In the lower right box, write the letter "B".
In the upper right box, draw a star.
In the lower left box, write the number "2".

In the upper left box, write the letter "V".
In the lower right box, draw a diamond.
In the upper right box, draw a crescent moon.
In the lower left box, write the number "6".

In the upper right box, write the letter "O".
In the lower left box, draw a smiley face.
In the upper left box, draw a lightning bolt.
In the lower right box, write the number "4".

In the upper left box, write the letter "F".
In the lower right box, draw a star.
In the upper right box, draw a lightning bolt.
In the lower left box, write the number "8".

Draw the hour hand in the correct position based on the hour indicated by the numeral below the clock.
Draw the minute hand in the correct position based on the number of minutes indicated by the numeral below the clock.

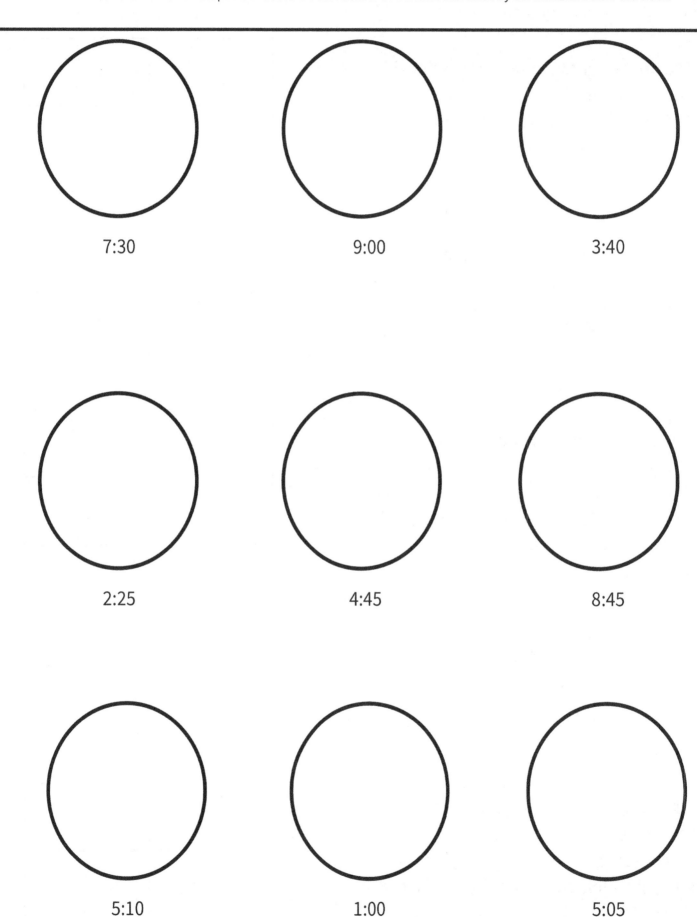

7:30

9:00

3:40

2:25

4:45

8:45

5:10

1:00

5:05

Temporal Awareness

Write the numerals and clock hands for the times listed below.

What time do you sleep?

When do you eat lunch?

When is dinner?

When do you wake up?

What time is it now?

When is your favorite TV show on?

When is your next meal?

What time did you go to bed last night?

What time was it 2 hours ago?

Made in the USA
Las Vegas, NV
22 January 2024

84737294R00092